MATT[illegible]

Biography

Memories of relationships and life ups and downs

Tina Louise Dixon

CONTENTS

CHAPTER 1

Another Generation Shot to Hell

Dad was a drinker as well. Every evening, he'd return home from whatever set he'd been on, or not, pour himself a large slug of vodka tonic, and declare, "This is the best thing that's happened to me all day." He was talking about a drink when he stated this. In Los Angeles, he is sitting on a couch with his son. Then he'd have four more before putting the fifth to bed. Dad also taught me a lot of valuable lessons. But he did teach me how to drink. It was no coincidence that my drink of choice was a double vodka tonic, and every time I thought, This is the best thing that happened to me all day. I saw my father drink six vodka tonics and still operate normally, so I believed it was doable. I assumed I'd be able to do the same. But there was something lurking in my shadows and genes, like a nasty beast in a dark spot, something I possessed that my father did not, and we wouldn't know what it was for another decade. Alcoholism, addiction, whatever you want to call it, I've decided to call it a Big Terrible Thing.

By 1986, I was convinced that celebrity would change everything, and I want it more than anyone else on the earth. It was exactly what I needed. It was the one thing that could make me whole again. I was sure of it. That evening, I asked my father what I should do. He was on his third vodka tonic, and he still had enough cogency in his tank to get a useful answer. He was getting irritated by the fact that my career was taking off; he wasn't jealous, but he was aware that I was younger than he was, that the road was rising to meet me, and that if I played my cards right, I might have a better career than he did. Having said that, he was always supportive—there was no "Great Santini" going on here. My father was my hero, and he was really proud of me.

"Well, Matty," he said, "can't hurt to call."

But no matter what my father said, I knew I'd contact that number. I'd suspected it from the moment I read the note. After all, this was Hollywood—that's how it's supposed to work, right? William Richert, it turned out, did not want to make a film in the back of a van. Richert had seen me perform for the ladies in the 101 that day and had watched enough of The Matthew Perry Show to want to cast me in a film based on his novel A Night in the Life of Jimmy Reardon. The novel and film are set in Chicago in the early 1960s; Reardon is a teenager who is being forced to go business school when all he really wants to do is save up enough money to fly to Hawaii to visit his love. I was cast as Reardon's best buddy, Fred Roberts, who, like Ed in Charles in Charge, was well-off and a little snobbish, as well as suffering from chronic virginity.

The film was shot in Chicago, so there I was, seventeen years old and on my way to the Windy City, sans parents, sans anything, an unaccompanied minor once more, but this time it seemed like liberation, like what I was born to do. I'd never been so ecstatic in my life. I fell completely in love with acting in Chicago, on this film, and with River Phoenix—and the icing on top of this profoundly amazing experience was that River and I became fast friends. Our film would eventually bomb at the box office, but that didn't matter. Even if it was just North Rush Street in cold Chicago, we'd been somewhere lovely and fantastic. And I knew that was the best experience of my life. My work was completed in approximately three weeks, but they (most likely River) liked me so much that they kept me on the film till the conclusion. Things didn't get any better after that. I cried again seven years later, on Halloween 1993, in front of the Viper Room in West Hollywood, when River died. (I heard screams from my apartment, went back to bed, and awoke to the news.) "The spirits of [River's] generation are being worn down," his mother wrote after his death, referring to drug usage, and by then, I was drinking every night. But it would be years before I realised what she meant.

I went back to LA from Chicago with Jimmy Reardon in the bag and returned to planet Earth in the guise of high school. I was still auditioning for a lot of stuff, but I wasn't getting anywhere. I was largely booking comedies, but I ended up guest starring on almost everything. My grades, though, remained dismal. I graduated with a 2.0 grade point average. My only request at my graduation was that both my mother and father attend, which they gladly fulfilled. The terribly awkward supper that followed appeared to just emphasise the notion that the child they shared was bound to be uncomfortable by default, despite being the funniest person in the room most of the time. But that night at dinner, I was just the third most attractive and third most funny. At the very least, a boyhood dream of theirs had come true, if only for one night, and even then, only in awkward silences and barbs handed back and forth like some angry cosmic joint.

I am grateful to my parents for attending that meal; it was a very sweet and utterly unneeded gesture on their part. However, it crystallised something for me that I had not expected. It seemed appropriate that they were not together. They would not be. They were correct to keep their distance. They both eventually met the person they were destined to be with. And I am overjoyed for both of them. Matty no longer needed to desire for his parents to be together. They wouldn't be in the same room together again for decades. Then, for a completely other purpose.

CHAPTER 2

Baggage

I first met Hank when I was sixteen. We were auditioning for a pilot starring Ellen Greene (from Little Shop of Horrors) on the CBS lot. He played my uncle in the pilot, and we both were cast. We got along so well that when it was time for me to leave the nest, I moved into a studio apartment in his building. I was drinking all the time—I spent my undergraduate years drinking at the Formosa—and I achieved a 4.0 GPA and was Alkoól Beta Kappa while drinking. My love of drink had truly taken command of my life.

Ten years later, I read in the Big Book of Alcoholics Anonymous, "Drinkers think they are trying to escape, but they are really trying to overcome a mental disorder they didn't know they had."

Someone finally understands me. But reading that was both fantastic and terrifying. It meant I wasn't alone—there were others who felt the same way I did—but it also meant I was an alcoholic who would have to stop drinking one day at a time for the rest of my life.

How could I ever have fun again?

Aside from my father's resentment, I had just scheduled my first TV show. I was seventeen years old and earning $5,000 every week. My ego was through the roof; I believed I was the shit, just as everyone else thought Second Chance was. It was ranked 93rd out of the ninety-three shows that season. After the first thirteen episodes, the Saint Peter / Blue Lighter thing was ignored, and the show basically followed myself and my friends on our different excursions. So it didn't matter that the show stayed 93rd on a list of 93rd—someone important had liked me enough to develop a show around me, which just boosted my ego to enormous levels. And it could have set me up for eventual success.

My father reacted with the news by missing every recording except the very last one. I assume he had his reasons.

As a result, I was able to land several guest roles following that, and two years later I was cast in another series, this time in a sitcom starring Valerie Bertinelli. Sydney followed Valerie's exploits as a private eye (!), and I played her fast-talking brother—that's all you'll ever need to know about those thirteen episodes (Sydney was cancelled after one half season). Despite the fact that it failed to captivate spectators, I'll never forget two things about Sydney.

First, Craig Bierko played Valerie's lawyer/love interest on the show—almost immediately after meeting Craig on set, I called Hank Azaria and said, "He sounds the way we do!" which was the finest praise I could offer someone. But before I could truly appreciate Craig's hilarity, there was the second thing I should tell you about Sydney: while filming, I fell madly in love with Valerie Bertinelli, who was clearly in a troubled marriage and clearly getting off on two of the funniest guys on the planet adoring her and heaping their attention on her.

Craig Bierko was the hottest thing in the 1994 pilot season. We were all auditioning for the latest batch of sitcoms and dramas, but Craig was the one everyone wanted. This, and he was faster with a line than I was. He was also far more attractive than me, but let's not get into that—we don't want a sobbing author on our hands. I should have despised him, but since laughter usually triumphs, I decided to keep loving him.

I was twenty-four, and I was already missing half of my auditions. As an actor, I was nearing the end of my career. The fight against auditions was being won slowly but steadily by drinking, and no one was really interested in me anyway. I wasn't getting any movie roles, and the ones I did get on TV weren't exactly ground-breaking. I was hungover half the time and on my way to lunch or the Formosa the rest of the time. One day, my manager sat me down and told me that the individuals I hoped to be—Michael Keaton, Tom Hanks—all exhibited the attitude I was aiming for. But they both looked fantastic, and he was getting daily criticism from casting directors and producers that I was a shambles.

Hank, too, began to worry that he was squandering his life and stopped coming to the Formosa and the amusing lunches—he was always serious about his body and his profession.

I shouldn't have been surprised, but around that time, my then-business manager called.

"Matthew, you are out of money."

"How about a little forewarning?" I was terrified, I said. "Did it occur to you that you could have given me a heads-up a few months ago?" You know, instead of waiting until I was broke, you might have called and said, 'Hey, Matthew, your funds are looking a little anaemic.'"

On the other end of the line, there was quiet, as if keeping track of someone's revenue before they went bankrupt was an altogether new concept for a business management. Fortunately, I had just enough energy to book a part in a bad pilot. After saying goodbye to my now-former business manager, I called my agents and told them I was out of money, needed a job, anything, and it had to be right away. If you're thinking that's how I got Friends, you might want to take a deep breath. That phone call led to the show that nearly prevented me from obtaining Friends.

L.A.X. 2194 was a "sci-fi comedy" about Los Angeles International Airport baggage handlers. You could stop there, but there's more: the numerals in the title reveal the twist: it's set two hundred years in the future, and the passengers are aliens. Ryan Stiles would play an automaton office manager with a strange accent (seriously, Ryan is a hilarious actor, but what was that accent?), and I would play the poor guy who had to be the lead in this mess and sort out the baggage issues for the arriving aliens, who happened to be played by Little People in ridiculous wigs.

If all of this sounds underwhelming, remember that it was far worse. For starters, I had to put on a futuristic shirt. Despite my reservations (remember, it was a "comedy" about baggage handlers set two hundred years in the future, with Little People playing the aliens), the pilot paid me $22,500, so I was set for drinks and meals at the Formosa for a while... But it also did something else: because I was linked to L.A.X. 2194, I was no longer available for any other shows.

Then calamity hit, and I don't mean L.A.X. 2194 being picked up for a season—thank God, that didn't happen. What did happen was that a script for a new show called Friends Like Us became the season's most popular read. Everyone who read it knew it was going to be fantastic; when I read it, I immediately called the same agents who had brought me L.A.X. 2194.

"You have to get me on Friends Like Us," I said.

"Not gonna happen," stated my agents. "You're a part of the baggage handlers' show." They've already taken your measurements for the futuristic clothing."

I was heartbroken. When I read the script for Friends Like Us, I felt as if someone had been following me around for a year, stealing my jokes, mimicking my mannerisms, and reproducing my world-weary yet hilarious outlook on life. One character in particular stuck out to me: it wasn't that I imagined myself as "Chandler," but that I was Chandler.

However, I also played Blaine in L.A.X. 2194. Is everyone lying to me? Am I the unluckiest person on the planet?

It only got worse from there. Because Friends Like Us was the season's hottest ticket, everyone was reading it, auditioning for it, and everyone, it seemed, decided that the role of Chandler was precisely like me and came to my flat to beg me to help them with their auditions. Based on my selections, a few even went a long way.Lunch was coming to an end, and Craig needed to inform his representatives where his head was at. Hank said his goodbyes and headed to the gym, as he always did, and I followed Craig as he looked for a pay phone. (There were no cell phones in 1994.) The nearest one was outside a Fred Segal store (which, oddly, also appears in my episode of Beverly Hills, 90210). Craig tossed a few cents into the machine, keyed in the numbers, and sat back to wait. They eventually patched him through.

Then I stood two feet away from Craig and watched him choose THE OTHER SHOW! I couldn't believe what I was hearing. So the new Best Friends leader and I parted ways. I dashed home to make another audition request for Friends Like Us.

I attended the taping of the pilot for Best Friends a few weeks later—it was amusing; Craig was funny, and he got the lead, which is what he really wanted. Perfectly fine, adorable show. However, the final character available during the whole 1994 pilot season, Chandler in Friends Like Us, remained uncast. I was still hooked on the fucking futuristic luggage handler show!

You know how the universe has plans for you that are difficult to believe, how the world wants something for you even if you've done everything you can to block that path?

Hello and welcome to my 1994.

Jamie Tarses, NBC producer, you will be missed. Jamie Tarses, who was working on NBC's Friends Like Us, allegedly turned to her then-husband, Fox TV producer Dan McDermott, one night in bed.

"Hey, is the show L.A.X. 2194 going to get picked up?" Jamie allegedly stated.

"No, it's awful—for starters, it's about baggage handlers in the year 2194," Dan remarked. They dress in futuristic vests..."

"Does Matthew Perry have any openings?" A secure second spot?" Jamie stated. (This is Hollywood jargon for "available.") (Incidentally, Jamie and I dated for several years after she divorced.)

A few days later, I received the phone call that would transform my life.

"You're meeting with Marta Kauffman about Friends Like Us tomorrow."

And I'm not lying when I say I knew how big it was all going to be right then and there.

Marta Kauffman was the person primarily responsible for Friends, along with David Crane. The next day, a Wednesday, I read as Chandler for her, and I broke every rule—for starters, I didn't bring any pages of the screenplay with me (you're meant to take the script with you when you read, because it shows the writers that it's still a work in progress). But at this point, I was so familiar with the script. Of course, I succeeded. The pilot season of 1994 had cast its final actor: Matthew Perry as Chandler Bing.

CHAPTER 3

Like I've Been There Before

It was so special that it felt like we'd all met before or something. Or maybe in another life, but definitely in this one. This was a memorable day. But that was the kind of day that dreams are built of. For the longest time, I didn't want to talk about Friends too much. Partly because I'd done lots of other things, but everyone always wanted to speak about Chandler—it's like James Taylor talking about "Fire and Rain" (a horrific little yarn if you've ever heard it). It's like a band has written a fantastic new album, but when they perform live, all everybody wants to hear are the hits. I've always respected Kurt Cobain's refusal to perform "Smells Like Teen Spirit," as well as Led Zeppelin's refusal to perform "Stairway to Heaven." According to the New York Times, "Friends... sticks to [Perry] like a sweaty shirt." They weren't wrong—in fact, that's simply fucking cruel—but they weren't the only ones who thought so. I was really good at something, but I was getting punished for it. Every Friday night, I left my blood, sweat, and tears onstage—we all did. And that should be a positive thing, not something that implies we can only excel at one thing.

I'm not going to complain. If you want to be typecast, this is the way to go. But in recent years, I've come to appreciate what Friends means to different people. And we understood right away that it was something very, very exceptional.

I was the last actor cast in the entire 1994 pilot season—in fact, I received the job on the final day of the season. With L.A.X. 2194 mercifully behind me, I was free to be Chandler Bing. The Monday after the Friday I was hired was day one of my new life—this was important, and I think we all sensed it because we all showed up on time. Matt LeBlanc was first every day, and Aniston was last every day. The cars improved, but the order remained unchanged.

We sat around the table, everyone meeting for the first time. Except for me and Jennifer Aniston. Jennifer and I had met three years before through mutual acquaintances. I was immediately taken with her (how could I not be?) and liked her, and I had the impression she was as well—maybe this was going to be something. Back then, I had two gigs in one day: Haywire, an America's Funniest Home Videos-style show, and a comedy. So I dialled Jennifer's number and told her, "You're the first person I wanted to tell this to!"

I could feel ice building through the phone, which was a bad decision. Looking back, it was evident that this gave her the impression that I liked her too much, or in the wrong way... and I just compounded the error by asking her out. She declined (which made going out with her tough), but stated she'd love to be friends with me, and I aggravated the situation by blurting, "We can't be friends!"

We became buddies a few years later, ironically. Fortunately, even though I was still attracted to her and thought she was fantastic, we were able to sail right past the past on that first day and focus on the fact that we had both received the best job Hollywood has to offer.

Everyone else was unfamiliar to me.

Courteney Cox was staggeringly lovely in a yellow gown. Lisa Kudrow had been recommended to me by a mutual acquaintance, and she was just as beautiful, witty, and highly smart as my friend had described. David Schwimmer had had his hair cut pretty short (he had been portraying Pontius Pilate for his theatre ensemble in Chicago) over his hangdog face and was incredibly entertaining right immediately; kind, witty, and inventive. He was the one who pitched the most jokes after me—I probably pitched 10 jokes a day and only two of them got in. They weren't just for me; I'd pitch them to everyone. "You know, it might be funny if you tried to say this..." I'd say to Lisa, and she'd try it.

Jimmy Burrows, the filmmaker, was also the greatest in the business, having directed Taxi and Cheers. He knew instinctively that getting to know each other and creating chemistry was Job One for us. There was instant energy in the air. I'd always wanted to be the only one who laughed. But now, at the age of twenty-four, I've understood that it's preferable if everyone is amusing. I could tell this was going to be enormous right away; I knew it from the start, but I didn't say anything. Part of this was due to the fact that it is not uncommon for an actor to screw up a table read so terribly that they were politely asked to leave before a single minute of shooting occurred. But that would have to wait until tomorrow; for now, Jimmy had taken the six of us to Monica's apartment set and ordered us to just talk to one another. So we talked and laughed about romance, our careers, our loves, and our losses. And the bond Jimmy had predicted would be crucial has begun.

On a gorgeous spring day, the six of us ate lunch together outside. "There are no stars here," Courteney, the group's lone established name at the time, said as we ate. This is a group performance. We're all meant to be friends."

Given her status—she'd appeared on Family Ties, Ace Ventura, Seinfeld, and had danced with Bruce Springsteen in the video for "Dancing in the Dark"—she could have been everything and everyone; she might easily have said, "I'm the star." She could have had her lunch someplace else and we'd have been cool with it. Instead, she simply stated, "Let's really work together and get to know each other." She stated it was what she'd noticed about how it worked on Seinfeld, and she hoped it would hold true for Friends as well. So we followed her advice. We were inseparable from the first morning. We shared every meal and played poker.... At first, I was full-on the joke man, cracking gags like a comedy machine whenever I could (probably to everyone's annoyance), trying to persuade everyone to like me because I was so hilarious.

Otherwise, why would anyone want me? It would take me fifteen years to realise that I didn't have to be a joke machine. We were allotted dressing rooms the first day, which didn't matter because we never used them. We were never apart. That first evening, when we all walked to our cars and said our goodbyes, I recall thinking, "I'm happy."

This was not an emotion I was accustomed to. That night, I called my pals (except for Craig Bierko, because of what had transpired) and told them what a fantastic day I'd had. As was my routine, I next spent another night "at college" (the Formosa). I recall stating that night that I was on a show that was better than anything I could have written myself.... My pals were all overjoyed for me, but I could sense a shift. Perhaps I was growing out of my Formosa phase? I had a life-changing job that required—nay, demanded—that I report to in the morning, so I drank significantly less than normal. My apartment even had a Lifecycle in the back, which I used every day, losing around ten pounds of baby/alcohol fat in the time between the pilot and the first episode.

I went to bed that night thinking, "I can't wait to get back there tomorrow." The next morning, as I drove from Sunset and Doheny over the Cahuenga Pass to the Warner Bros. lot in Burbank, I saw myself leaning against the windshield. I really wanted to be there.

That will be the case for the next decade. Day two was big. We reported to a new building—Building 40—for our first table read. I was nervous and excited, and yet confident, too. I had always been good at table reads. But there was still the looming thought that anyone could be fired and replaced (Lisa Kudrow, for example, had originally been cast as Roz on Frasier but had been fired during the rehearsal process by none other than ... Friends director, Jimmy Burrows). If jokes didn't land, or something was off, well, anybody could be replaced before they'd even properly found their way to their dressing room.

But I knew Chandler. I could shake hands with Chandler. I was him. That day, the room was packed—in fact, it was standing room only. There were writers, executives, and network people. There must have been a hundred people in the room, but I was a song-and-dance man, and this is where I excelled. We got reacquainted with Marta Kauffman, David Crane, and Kevin Bright—the people behind the show, and who had hired us—and almost instantly we all felt they were our parental figures. Before the table read began, we all went around the room introducing ourselves and saying what we did for the show. Then it was time to read. How would it go? Would the chemistry we'd only just started to create show up, or were we just six young hopefuls making believe that this would be our big break?

We needn't have worried—we were ready, the universe was ready. We were pros—the lines flew out of our mouths. No one made a mistake. All the jokes landed. We finished to thunderous applause.

Everyone could smell money. The cast could smell fame.

After the read the six of us piled into a van and were brought to the actual set at stage 24 to begin rehearsing. But it was the run-through at the end of the day that sealed the deal—the jokes, the chemistry, the script, the direction, everything was magical. All the elements seemed to meld into one hilarious, cogent, powerful whole. And we all knew it.

This show was going to work, and it was going to change everyone's lives forever. I swear there was a popping sound; if you listened really closely, you could hear it. It was the sound of people's dreams coming true. It was everything I thought I wanted. I was going to fill all the holes with Friends Like Us. Fuck Charlie Sheen. I was going to be so famous that all the pain I carried with me would melt like frost in sunlight; and any new threats would bounce off me as though this show was a force field I could cloak myself in.

In show business, there is an unwritten rule that to be humorous, you must either look funny or be older. But here we were, six attractive people in their twenties, all delivering hilarious jokes.

I drove home on a cloud that evening. There was no traffic; all of the traffic signals were green; and a drive that should have lasted half an hour took fifteen minutes. The attention that I had always felt eluded me was going to flood every part of my existence, like a burst of lightning. People were starting to like me. I was going to be sufficient. I was important. I wasn't overly needy. I was a celebrity.

Nothing was going to go in our way now. No one entering a ballroom would have to turn around and look at me. Not the lovely woman walking three feet in front of me, but all eyes would be on me now.

We practised for the rest of the week, and it was then that we noticed something else. That had never happened to me as an actor before or since, and it was beautiful: the employers were not in the least tyrannical. In reality, it was a very creative environment. We could pitch jokes, and the best one would win, regardless of where it originated from. What did the craft services lady say that was amusing? It didn't matter where you put it. So I was there not only as an actor, but also as a creative force.

The creators also took each of us out to lunch to get to know us better so that they could add some of our true personalities into the show. At lunch, I mentioned two things: first, that while I did not consider myself unattractive, I had awful luck with women and my relationships tended to be disastrous; and second, that I was not comfortable in quiet at all—I had to break every such time with a joke. because this became an opportunity for Chandler Bing to be funny—ideal for a sitcom—because Chandler wasn't much good with women, either (as he shouts to Janice as she leaves his apartment, "I've scared ya; I've said too much; I'm awkward and hopeless and desperate for love!").

Consider a better sitcom character: someone who is uncomfortable with silence and must break it with a joke.

This was all too true for both Chandler and me. I knew early on in the production of Friends that I still had a huge crush on Jennifer Aniston. Our greetings and farewells were awkward. And then I'd wonder, "How long can I look at her?" Is three seconds excessive?

But that shadow vanished in the blazing light of the show. (That, and her utter lack of enthusiasm.)

Nobody made a mistake on tape nights. We might have skipped a scene if a joke didn't land—all the writers would huddle and rewrite—but errors? It simply never happened. Many shows feature blooper reels, but Friends has only a handful. From the pilot on... in fact, that pilot was flawless. We were the New York Yankees from the start: slick, professional, and on top of our game. We were prepared.

And I was speaking in a way that no one had ever spoken in a sitcom before, hitting weird emphases, picking a word in a sentence that you would not think was the beat, employing the Murray-Perry Cadence. I didn't realise it at the time, but my way of speaking would permeate the society over the next few decades—for now, I was just trying to find fascinating ways into phrases that were already humorous, but that I believed I could genuinely make dance. (Marta Kauffman subsequently said that the writers would underline the word that wasn't generally emphasised in a sentence just to see what I'd do with it.)

Even when there were problems with the characters, we were able to work things out to the point where the answers were legendary in their own right. I realised the script was unique when I first read it because it was so character-driven and intelligent. But Matt LeBlanc was worried early on that because he was portrayed as a suave, macho ladies' man in the script, Rachel, Monica, and Phoebe wouldn't be friends with him, wouldn't like him all that much, making his role less believable.

It didn't help that Matt was quite attractive—he had leading man features, which made me a little jealous when I first saw him. But he was so charming and humorous that whatever envy I felt quickly vanished—but he still hadn't found the perfect route into his role. He was the one character in the program who hadn't been fully defined—he was portrayed as a cool, Pacino-type, out-of-work actor, so he was acting it that way, but it wasn't working. During a wardrobe session, he wore brown leather pants, which were thankfully rejected by everyone, particularly Marta, who was in control.

Then there's the scene early in the film where he talks to Courteney about a woman he's been seeing and how the sex isn't working out. Courteney asks him whether he's considered being there for the girl, and Joey simply doesn't get it. That's when he went from a ladies' guy to a lovable, useless, dumb puppy. He emphasised this by making a running joke about things being repeated to him and him not paying attention. He'd identified his role on the show, which was essentially that of a big dumb brother to Rachel, Monica, and Phoebe. Everyone was in their proper place.

Matt would come into my dressing room on occasion, mostly during season one, and ask me how to say his lines. And I'd tell him, and he'd walk downstairs and nail it... but he wins Most Improved Player because, by season ten, I was going into his room and asking him how he'd pronounce some of my lines.

This was only the beginning. For the time being, we were filming shows in preparation for our fall 1994 air date. And no one knew who we were yet.

With the shows completed, all that remained was to determine our time slot. NBC felt they had something unique on their hands, so they sandwiched us between Mad About You and Seinfeld. It was the ideal location; plum. Because this was before streaming, your time slot was critical. It was still the days of appointment television, when people would rush home to see the 8:00 or 9:00 p.m. show. And people planned their life around their shows rather than the other way around. So 8:30 p.m. on a Thursday between two enormous performances was a tremendous deal.

We took the Warner Bros. aircraft to New York for the "upfronts." The upfronts are the presentations of a show to the affiliates. On this trip, they informed us that the show's name had been changed to Friends (when they renamed it, I thought it was a terrible idea—I never said I was a smart person), and Friends was a smash with the affiliates as well—everything was falling into place. We were celebrating, getting drunk, and partying in New York before heading to Chicago for more upfronts and partying.

Then we had to wait another summer before the show debuted. That summer was remarkable for three things: gambling in Vegas at Jimmy Burrows' request, a solo trip to Mexico, and a make-out session in a closet with Gwyneth Paltrow.

When I met Gwyneth, I was back in Williamstown, Massachusetts. She was there for a play, and I was there to see my grandfather. We went into a broom cupboard and made out at a big party. We were both still unknown enough that it didn't make it into the headlines, so it was up to Jimmy Burrows to give me a reality check.

After the upfronts, it was clear that the show was going to be a hit, so Jimmy flew us all to Vegas on the jet—we watched the pilot of Friends on the way—and once there, he gave us each $100 and told us to go gamble and have fun, because we'd never be able to do it again once the show aired in the fall.

"Your lives are going to change completely," Jimmy warned, "so do some things in public now because once you're as famous as you're about to be, you won't be able to do them again." And that's exactly what we did: we six new friends got drunk, gambled, and wandered through the casinos, just six close strangers on a weekend trip, unknown to anyone, no one asking for autographs or photos, none of us being pursued by paparazzi, a million miles away from what was to come, which was every single moment of our lives being documented in public for all to see forever.

I still desired fame, but I could detect a strange flavour in the air—would fame, that elusive lover, truly fill all the gaps I carried about with me? What if I couldn't put twenty on black in a dimly lit casino with a vodka tonic in my hand without someone shouting, "Matthew Perry just put twenty on black, everyone, come and see!" This was the final summer of my life when I could make out with a gorgeous young woman named Gwyneth at a party and no one cared except Gwyneth and I.

Is the payout worthwhile? Would giving up a "normal" existence be worth the price of people searching through my trash and photographing me at my worst, best, and all in between?

Would I ever be able to replicate anonymously my twenty-first birthday, when I'd drunk seven 7 and 7s, poured a bottle of wine into a huge brandy snifter—you know, the one they put on the piano for tips—ordered a cab, gotten into the back of the cab with the snifter, still sipping the wine, tried to give directions to my home when I could only pronounce the letter L, only for the guy up front to

Most importantly, will these gaps be filled? Would I want to swap places with David Pressman or Craig Bierko, or vice versa? What would I tell them if my name became slang for stand-up comedians and late-night hosts, slang that signified "addict"? What would I say if strangers loathed me, adored me, and everything in between?

What would I say to them?

And what would I say to God if he reminded me of my prayer, which I'd said three weeks before I met Friends?

You can do whatever you want to me, God. Please, please, please make me famous. He was ready to fulfil one side of the contract, which meant he could do whatever he wanted with me as the other half. I was utterly at the mercy of a God who was kind at times and believed it was absolutely fine to hang his own son on a fucking cross at others. Which path would he take for me? Which would Saint Peter choose? Which is better: gold, red, or blue?

I suppose I was about to learn. With Jimmy Burrows' warnings of future fame still echoing in my head, I decided to make one last trip as an anonymous individual.

I travelled to Mexico by myself late in the summer of 1994. I'd recently split up with Gaby and decided to go on a booze cruise by myself. I strolled around Cabo, getting drunk and calling girls in LA from my room. Then, every night on the trip, I'd go to some strange party where everyone was frightened until they handed out a jug of booze, at which point it was all over. I was lonely, I hadn't gotten laid, and it was hot in Cabo but frigid inside me. I could feel God watching and waiting for me. The most terrifying thing was that I thought God was omniscient, which meant he already knew what he had in store for me.

However, when Decca's A&R man Dick Rowe turned down the Beatles, he told Brian Epstein in 1961 that "guitar groups are on their way out." I'm curious how those reviewers feel now that they've trashed perhaps the greatest beloved program of all time. They completely missed the mark on that one. Did they despise Seinfeld as well? M*A*S*H? Cheers? What about St. Elsewhere?

We weren't about to leave. We were the epitome of prime time, back when prime time still mattered. The television gold rush. Even more crucial than the positive reviews was the fact that we had only lost around 20% of the crowd for Mad around You, which was an exceptionally strong result for a new production. We were beating Mad About You by episode six, indicating that we were a tremendous hit. We quickly rose to the top ten, then the top five, and we would remain there for the next decade. This is still unheard of. So there you have it—fame. Friends were tremendous, just as we predicted, and I couldn't endanger that. I adored my co-stars, the writing, everything about the program... but I was also suffering with addictions, which contributed to my sense of humiliation. I had a secret that no one knew about. Even producing the shows could be difficult. "I felt like I was going to die if [the live audience] didn't laugh," I said at the 2020 reunion. And it's undoubtedly unhealthy. But every now and then, I'd say something and they wouldn't laugh, and I'd sweat and—and just go into convulsions. I'd freak out if I didn't get the chuckle I was intended to get. Every night I felt like that."

This pressure had put me in a terrible mood, and I also knew that just one of the six individuals working on the event was sick. But the recognition I craved had arrived—in London, it was as if we were the Beatles, with crowds screaming outside our hotel rooms—and the performance ended up touring the world.

I travelled to New York in late October 1995, between the airings of episodes five and six of season two, to make my first appearance on the Late Show, when being on Letterman was the pinnacle of pop culture celebrity. I was dressed in a black suit, and Letterman would point to my lapel and say, "late 1960s, British Invasion, kinda mod."

"Ladies and gentlemen, this man is on the number one show in America, please welcome Matthew Perry."

I walked out a celebrity. I'd made it. But I was so scared that I couldn't stand, so I was relieved to be sitting. I shook Mr. Letterman's hand and launched into my well-rehearsed routine, a lengthy recap of a typical Gilligan's Island episode. I managed to tell the identical story to Yasser Arafat, who was staying in my hotel (it was the UN's fiftieth anniversary, and everyone was in town). This was the kind of strange, wordy story Letterman enjoyed. The laughs came, and I even got Dave to crack a few times, and my earth-shattering fear was well masked.

Everything was in order. Everything was perfect. I had just turned twenty-five years old. I was in the world's largest sitcom; I was in a hotel in New York, watching as world leaders were rushed into elevators by security forces, putting on a thousand-dollar suit before joshing it up with Dave Letterman.

This was a celebrity. And God peered down on me, just beyond the glare of the city, past the skyscrapers and the faint stars sparkling beyond the midtown skies. He has all of the time in the world. He invented time, fuck. He'd never forget. Something was on the horizon. I had an idea what it was, but I wasn't positive. Something about drinking every night... But exactly how awful could it get? But the juggernaut was only getting started. The show was a cultural touchstone; we were swamped everywhere we went (David Schwimmer would later describe the story of being approached on the street by a swarm of young ladies who physically pushed his fiancée out of the way to get near him). I also had a new, and very famous, girlfriend by late 1995, right around the time of the Letterman performance. But before we get there, I have to settle some business with the "other" Chandler.

I didn't hear from Craig Bierko for two years after I got Chandler—he had moved to New York, and we lost touch.

Best Friends, the show he chose over Friends Like Us, had gone nowhere. (Later, Warren Littlefield, former network president of

NBC, wrote in his memoir about Craig not choosing Friends, "Thank God! There was something called Snidely Whiplash about Craig Bierko. He seemed to have a lot of anger underneath. The attractive leading man who you love and can do comedy is very rare.") He was working steadily—he'd eventually star in The Music Man on Broadway and The Long Kiss Goodnight with Geena Davis and Sam Jackson, among a lot of other really awesome stuff—but the divergence of our fortunes had left our friendship in flames.

I missed him. He was still the quickest comedic mind I'd ever met, and I loved that—and much else—about him. I could no longer go to the Formosa to just hang out, either; I missed that life, too. I'd taken to drinking alone in my apartment because that was safest. The illness was deepening, but I couldn't see it, not then. And if anyone saw how much I was drinking, they might be alarmed and ask me to stop. And stopping was, of course, impossible.

One day, though, Craig Bierko called me out of the blue. He wanted to come by and see me. I was delighted, but apprehensive. You know that feeling when you end up dating someone your best friend had a crush on? It felt like that; I'd taken the role he could and should have taken, and everything had gone gold for me, then platinum, then some other rare metal as yet undiscovered.

I had no idea how a meeting with my former friend would go. Marta Kauffman would later comment, "We saw a countless number of actors [for Chandler], but things happened as they were supposed to happen." But I couldn't say anything like that to Craig, because the thing that was supposed to happen—the miracle—had happened to me, not to him. (That had been his choice, not mine.)

When he got to my apartment, the tension was high. Craig spoke first.

"I want you to know that I am very sorry for not speaking to you for two years," he said. "I simply could not handle that you got rich and famous doing a role that I turned down. We were both good enough to get that role, and yeah, so, I just could not handle it…."

I heard him out; there was silence. The traffic on Sunset was backing up all the way to the Fred Segal on La Cienega.

I decided I wouldn't mention Fred Segal.

I hated what I was actually about to say, but I had to say it.

I said: "You know what, Craig? It doesn't do what we all thought it would. It doesn't fix anything." (What a sobering thought for a twenty-six-year-old who had only ever wanted fame and had only just realised that fame hadn't filled the holes at all. No, what had filled the holes was vodka.) Craig stared at me; I don't think he believed me; I still don't think he believes me. I think you actually have to have all of your dreams come true to realise they are the wrong dreams.

Later, when I was promoting Studio 60 on the Sunset Strip, I told The Guardian, "I've been on the least-watched show in the history of television [Second Chance, in 1987] and the most-watched [Friends] and none of it really did what I thought it was going to do to my life."

Given everything, there is no way I wouldn't change places with Craig, and David Pressman, and the guy in the gas station down the block—I'd change places with all of them in a minute, and forever, if only I could not be who I am, the way I am, bound on this wheel of fire. They don't have a brain that wants them dead. They slept fine at night. I don't expect that would make them feel any better about the choices they made, the way their lives went. I would give it all up not to feel this way. I think about it all the time; it's no idle thought—it's a coldhearted fact. That Faustian prayer I made was a stupid one, the prayer of a child. It was not based on anything real. But it became real. I have the money, the recognizability, and the near-death experiences to prove it.

CHAPTER 4

No Fourth Wall

You know how some folks felt like they were living the same day over and over again throughout Covid? This is the day I wish I could relive (this is the Groundhog Day of my Groundhog Day). In fact, I wish I could go back in time and relive it every day for the rest of my life. But I'm afraid I can't. So the only way to get past that is to tell it as a tale and see if it helps.

Taos, New Mexico, New Year's Eve 1995. We'd been playing football in the snow all afternoon. Julia Roberts, my girlfriend, and a slew of our pals. She was the biggest movie star in the world, and I was on the most popular television show.

Initially, the wooing was done via fax. A two-foot-long courtship, full with poems and flights of imagination and two gigantic stars falling for each other and uniting in a lovely, romantic way, exists somewhere in the globe. I was walking on air at the time. Nothing could touch me since I was at the centre of it all. I continued sliding my hand into the white-hot flame of fame, but it didn't burn yet; it was the inert centre. I hadn't realised yet that celebrity would not fill the need, but it did at the time, thank you very much.

Friends' first season had been a big hit, and I had practically drifted into season two. I'd done Letterman and was scheduled to do Leno. We'd graced the covers of People and Rolling Stone magazines when both were huge. Now the film offers were pouring in. Why wouldn't they? I was receiving whatever I wanted. A million-dollar film offer here, a million-dollar film offer there. I wasn't Julia Roberts, but there were only a few of us.

Then something only celebrities experience occurred. Marta Kauffman contacted me and suggested that I deliver flowers to Julia Roberts.

Do you mean the universe's biggest star, Julia Roberts?

"Sure, great, but why?" I said.

Julia had been offered the post-Super Bowl episode in season two, but she would only do the program if she could be a part of my plot line. Let me state it again: she would only do the program if she could be a part of my plot. (Was I having a good or bad year?) But first, I needed to entice her.

I deliberated for a long time about what to write on the card. I wanted it to sound professional from start to finish. (Star to much larger star.) But I also wanted something flirtatious in there to complement what she had said. I'm still proud of the decision I made. The only thing more thrilling than the thought of you appearing on the show is that I finally have a reason to give you flowers. Isn't that good? I was terrified to sleep at night, but I could turn on the charm when needed. But my work here isn't done yet. Her response was that she'd agree to be on the show if I fully explained quantum physics to her. Wow. First and foremost, I'm having an argument with the woman who developed lipstick, and I need to get back to work.

The next day, I emailed her a paper about wave-particle duality, the uncertainty principle, and entanglement, only some of which was metaphorical. Many years later, Alexa Junge, a staff writer on the program, told The Hollywood Reporter, "[Julia] was interested in [Matthew] from afar because he's so charming." There was a lot of flirtation going on around faxing. She was filling out questionnaires for him, such as, 'Why should I go out with you?' And everyone in the writers' room pitched in to help him explain why. He could get by without us, but there was no doubt we were on Team Matthew and working hard to make it happen for him."

All of our efforts paid off in the end. Julia not only agreed to go on the show, but she also sent me a gift: bagels—many and lots of bagels. Yes, why not? Julia Roberts was there.

Thus began a three-month fax-based courtship. This was pre-internet, pre-cell phones, and all of our communication was done via fax. And there were hundreds of them. At first, it was on the outside of romance: I sent her poems, asked her to identify the Los Angeles Kings' triple title line, and so on. And it's not like we weren't both busy—I was filming the most popular program on the globe, and she was in France filming a Woody Allen film, Everyone Says I Love You. (She was, of course.) But three or four times a day, I'd sit by my fax machine, watching the piece of paper gently unfold to show her next missive. I was so pleased that some evenings I'd find myself at a party, having a flirting dialogue with a beautiful woman, and then cutting the conversation short so I could run home and see if a new fax had arrived. One had nine times out of 10. They were so clever—the way she wove sentences together, the way she saw the world, the way she conveyed her own thoughts. It wasn't uncommon for me to read these faxes three, four, or even five times while smirking at the paper like a lunatic. It seemed as if she had been sent to this planet to make everyone happy, including me. I was giddy as a fifteen-year-old on his first date.

And we'd never even spoken before, let alone met. Something changed early one morning. Julia's fax was sweet. "I'm in over my head," I confessed to a friend. You must come over immediately. Please correct me if I'm wrong."

I handed him the fax when he came, and he remarked, "Yup, you're not wrong." You're clearly in over your head."

"What exactly am I supposed to send back?"

"Well, how do you feel?"

"Oh, fuck off," I retorted, "just tell me what to say."

So "Cyrano" and I put together and sent a fax that was also romantic. Then we stood there, looking at each other, by the fax machine. Two males are simply staring at a machine.

The jarring sound of the fax machine—all bongs and whirls and hissing messages from outer space—filled my apartment after roughly 10 minutes. It said, "Call me," and her phone number was at the bottom. I grabbed the phone and dialled Julia Roberts' number. I was as nervous as I had been since my first appearance on Letterman. But the talk was easy—I made her laugh, and what a laugh it was.... She was obviously incredibly intelligent. I could tell right away that she was easily in the top three storytellers I'd ever met. Her anecdotes were so brilliant, in fact, that I asked her whether she had planned them ahead of time. As we drew to a conclusion after five and a half hours, I realised I wasn't nervous any longer. We couldn't stop talking after that—five-hour chats here, four-hour conversations there. We were falling; I wasn't sure where we were falling, but we were falling. We were clearly in severe trouble. My phone rang again one Thursday.

"I'll be there at two p.m. on Saturday."

Click.

And there you have it.

How did she find out where I lived? What if she disliked me? What if the faxes and phone calls were all cute, but in real life, she didn't want me anymore? Why can't I give up drinking? That Saturday, at 2:00 p.m., there was a knock on my door. Matty, take a deep breath. When I opened it, there she was, Julia Roberts, smiling on the other side. I think I remarked something along the lines of, "Oh, that Julia Roberts."

Even at times like this, the jokes raced past. Craig would have said it faster if he had been present. She laughed like Julia Roberts, the kind of laugh that can launch a thousand ships. And any stress appeared to vanish. She inquired as to how I was doing.

"I feel like the luckiest man on the planet." "How are things going?"

"You should probably invite me inside right now."

I did let her in, both metaphorically and actually, and a connection blossomed. We'd already be dating by the time we began filming the Friends Super Bowl episode.

But it was New Year's Eve in Taos when we shot it. It was the year 1996. Julia Roberts was my girlfriend. I'd even met her parents. She drove me there in her orange Volkswagen Beetle after I had flown there privately. I assumed I had money. She was wealthy.

We'd spent the entire day playing football in the snow. Julia afterwards looked at me, checked her watch—11:45 p.m.—took my hand in hers, and said, "Come with me."

We climbed a mountain in this large blue vehicle, snow swirling around us. I didn't know where we were headed. We appeared to be ascending into the very stars themselves. We eventually arrived at a peak, where the clouds parted and we could see New Mexico and beyond, all the way back to Canada. She made me feel like the ruler of the world as we sat there. The year 1996 began with a moderate snowfall.

Julia appeared on Letterman in February, and he grilled her on whether or not we were dating. She has recently appeared as a guest star in the Friends episode "The One After the Super Bowl." That program, which featured guest performers such as Julia, Jean-Claude Van Damme, Brooke Shields, and Chris Isaak, among others, was watched by 52.9 million people, making it the most watched show ever to follow a Super Bowl. The ad income alone was staggering—more than $500,000 for thirty seconds of television. The show was now firmly established as NBC's main cash cow.

(However, I recall thinking a few nights ago, "I wish I was in the ER instead of Friends." I was always the centre of attention. The issue remained, my fingerprint, the hue of my eyes.)

Julia's segment of the double episode was shot a few days after New Year's, from January 6 to 8. "Back then, I used humour as a defence mechanism—thank God I don't do that anymore," they'd wrote, adding "I've met the perfect woman." Our couch kiss was so lifelike that everyone assumed it was real. It was. She was fantastic on the show, and our chemistry seemed to permeate televisions across the country.

"Yes, I've been going out with Matthew Perry, and for some reason, maybe because I did the Super Bowl show, people think it's the Matthew Perry from Friends," Julia said in response to Letterman. But it's actually this haberdasher I met in Hoboken. But Matthew Perry from Friends is very nice, so I don't mind."

She also described me as "awfully clever, funny, and handsome."

Everything was a yes back then. After we finished season two, I flew to Las Vegas to shoot my first major film in April. I was paid a million dollars to appear in Fools Rush In alongside Salma Hayek. It's still one of my favourite films. If I were making that movie now, I would travel with three other people, primarily because I am afraid of being alone. But it was just me back then. I wasn't filled with fear as I am today. That, I believe, is why they send young people to war. They are youthful; they are fearless; they are unstoppable.

Don't get me wrong: I was scared to make Fools Rush In. I was in Vegas, carrying a $30 million film on my shoulders. On the first day, I was driving home and told the driver, "You have to pull over." He did, and I threw up on the side of the road in panic. On film, not only is the process slower, but it also only works if you truly feel what you're attempting to depict as a feeling. This deeper work can be tough to transfer to, and I found it especially difficult because sequences in movies are often shot out of order. On day two of Fools Rush In, we were filming a scene at the obstetrician's office, and I recall hearing our baby's heartbeat for the first time. Given that I'd only recently met Salma, I had no idea how to acquire a feel for it. Later on, I recall a situation that made me want to cry. That made me nervous as well. I had been thinking about it all day and worried about it all night. I managed to pull it off somehow. The approach is simple: think of anything that makes you sad. However, timing is tricky because you must perform it at precisely the proper time and over and over again. I'd been crying all day on the set of Fools Rush In. "We've been doing this for ten hours, man," I told Andy Tennant, the director. "I have nothing left in me."

Andy stated, "We need it two more times, buddy."

I fell into tears at the thought of it. We both chuckled and agreed that there had to be something else in the tank. (Actually, serious acting is simpler for me than funny acting. When I see a scene, I think, "I don't have to be funny?" This will be a breeze. So far in my career,

I've been nominated for four Emmys. There is one in comedy and three in drama.)

But I was starting to think of some fascinating ways to tap into real emotions and be more of a leading man than a witty sitcom actor. There is a large firework show around noon at the Stratosphere building in Vegas—I urged Salma to look at the building then since that is how my character felt when he first met her character. Salma had also tried her hardest—at the outset of the shoot, she came into my trailer and said, "Let's just spoon a little bit."

"Oh, OK!" I responded, doing my best Chandler impression of a double-take and a cynical stare. Let's only spoon a small amount!"

Salma was often coming up with complex and lengthy ideas about how to conduct a scene, but her long-winded ideas weren't always helpful. There's one scene where I confess my love for her. She recommended that instead of looking at each other, we should gaze ahead at our future together. After approximately twenty minutes of listening to this foolishness, I eventually said: "Listen, Salma," I said, "I'm telling you I love you in this scene." You can look wherever you like, but I'll be gazing at you."

I went over the script and pitched gags to Andy Tennant, who was a really smart and extremely pleasant person, during the film's production. He sat on me—I was hopping around doing my silly little things—and he'd pull me aside and say, "You don't have to do that." You're intriguing enough to keep an eye on without doing that."

That line of thought enabled him to coax one of the best performances of my career from me. Could this be another way of expressing Matty, you're enough, the words I've wanted to hear my entire life? (Andy went on to direct scores of films, including Hitch, which starred Will Smith. I assume nice folks don't finish last.) Andy was also willing to listen to propose ideas. My friend Andrew Hill Newman was visiting me on set one day when he said, "You are everything I never knew I always wanted." I wrote it down and gave it to Andy Tennant, who loved it, and it became the movie's most famous phrase. And perhaps the best line I've ever said in a movie.

One day while shooting, I noticed a group of people on Jet Skis in the background on Lake Mead, and I asked if I might ride one during the lunch break. But this was the beginning of the film, and I was warned that it was too dangerous.

But everything was a yes back then, so I just said, "Erm, you have to say yes to that."

So I went out on Lake Mead. The sun was shining brightly, and the blue water crackled like a flame. As I sped about on the Jet Ski, I could see the Hoover Dam in the distance, where the movie's conclusion would be shot, and Mount Wilson towering over everything like a warning. But in my life, everything was wonderful. I had the most gorgeous, famous woman in the world as my girlfriend; I was on America's number one TV show; and I was making a lot of money filming a movie that could only be a box-office smash. I cranked up the Jet Ski, feeling the loose-soft connection to the water, twisting this way and that, the chop knocking me up and down on the seat, my right hand turning and turning and turning, pushing that machine to its limit.

Then I turned the Jet Ski sharply right, while my body continued straight ahead. I was in the air, and then I wasn't. When I surfaced, I looked back to where I'd begun, and there stood forty people on the shoreline, the entire crew, who had been watching me risk my life throughout the film, and who had now all jumped into Lake Mead to retrieve me. I knew I was harmed when I got back to shore. That night, there was a big scene to shoot—the delivery of the kid, the pivotal moment—and I had to be there. But everything hurt, and I had really messed up my neck. The crew recognized my distress and summoned a doctor, who stopped by my trailer and delivered me a single medication in a plastic container.

"Take this when you're done," advised the doctor. "Everything will be just fine."

I kept the medication in my pocket, and I swear to God, if I hadn't taken it, none of the events of the next three decades would have happened the way they did. Who can say? I only know it was terrible.

In Fools Rush In, my character is a real estate entrepreneur who drives a red Mustang. The action lasted all night, but we finished just before daybreak. The sun was getting closer to the horizon.

"Hey, do you think I can drive that Mustang back to Vegas?" I inquired.

I'm astonished that they said yes to anything straight after the Jet Ski incident. They did, however. When I left the parking lot, the first light of the Nevada day was seeping over Mount Wilson. I lowered the top of that Mustang and consumed the pill. I thought of Julia; I imagined myself flying above Lake Mead, carefree. I reflected on my childhood, but it didn't bother me at the time. Something clicked in me when the drug kicked in. And it's been that click that I've been looking for for the rest of my life. I reflected on Craig Bierko, the Murray brothers, and Friends. Summer was approaching, with its pink cirrus clouds and gentle, arid air. My pink sky looked like this. If a locomotive struck me, I would just turn to the engineer and remark, "It happens, brother." I was lying in the grass in my backyard in Canada, surrounded once more by Murray puke. I couldn't believe how great I felt; I was completely and utterly euphoric. The medication had replaced my blood with warm honey in my body. I felt like I was on top of the world. It was the most amazing sensation I'd ever felt. Nothing could possibly go wrong. I recall thinking as I drove that red Mustang convertible to my leased house in Vegas, "If this doesn't kill me, I'm doing it again." Of course, this is a negative memory because of what happened thereafter, but it was also a good memory. That morning, I felt near to God. I had experienced heaven, something not many people do. That morning, I shook God's hand. Was it God or was it someone else? When I came home that morning, my first thought was to contact that doctor and inform him that the tablet had relieved my agony (I decided to leave out the God bit). When I went to bed, forty more of those tablets had been brought to my residence. Eureka!

Be cautious, Matty; something that feels so pleasant must have consequences. I'm aware of the implications now, and boy, am I aware of them. But I didn't know them at the time. I wish that was the end of my thoughts on Fools Rush In. Fun insider anecdotes on how movies are made. I hate to bust the celebrity-industrial complex bubble, but there are real people behind the glitz and martini shots and A-cameras. What no one could see was that someone's life, most likely the least probable candidate, was about to plunge through the gates of hell. After a year and a half, I was taking 55 of those medications every day. My life was in shambles when I entered Hazelden recovery in Minnesota, weighing 128 pounds. I was terrified, convinced I was going to die, and had no idea what had happened to me. I wasn't looking to die; I just wanted to feel better. Of course, the fact that "Matthew Perry is in rehab" became a major news issue. I wasn't even given the chance to hash out my difficulties in private. Everyone was aware. It was on the covers of every magazine—I didn't even have the obscurity that everyone else did. I was scared. I was also young, so I recovered quickly. I was back on my feet and looking healthy in twenty-eight days. This was also a significant news story, although nowhere near as enormous as the other one.

Making movies is a very different beast than making television. If you were sad about something on Friends, you'd play it up as if you were the saddest person in the world—basically, for the back row of the live audience. Your performance also has a wink to the audience, as if to say, "Hey, everybody, watch this." You're going to love it." Every week on a sitcom, it's like performing a one-act play. There are 300 individuals in the crowd, and you must open up to them.

Film production moves at a considerably slower pace—there's a master shot, a closeup, and then an even closer closeup. And if your character was depressed, you portrayed him depressed. There was no winking—these were the professionals, baby. On Friends, however, we practised rapidly. "You guys are going so fast!" Alec Baldwin once said as a guest star. We had guest stars all the time, which meant we had to think on our feet all the time. Sean Penn was one of my favourites in season eight, appearing in two episodes and nailing it. I said at the end of the table read, "I've always dreamed of working with Sean Penn, but I never thought I'd have to wear a pink bunny rabbit suit to do so."

Friends never shattered the metaphorical fourth wall, despite the absence of an actual fourth wall in the apartment. The closest we ever came was with Sean, when I pitched a tag (the little conclusion scene after the main tale has aired) in which I was backstage in the bunny rabbit outfit. "Sean, can I talk to you for a second?" I ask as he walks by.

"Sure, Matthew, what's up?"

"Well, I've been really thinking about this. And I believe you are the right person to talk to about this." As I say this, I'm smoking, and as I extinguish the cigarette with my gigantic bunny foot, I remark, "I've been looking to transition myself into dramatic work."

Sean Penn examines me for almost five beats before saying, "Good luck."

The table read got a good laugh out of it. But it breached a rule that we hadn't broken in five years. Even someone as powerful as Sean Penn and me dressed ridiculously in a large pink bunny costume couldn't break the fourth wall. It remained in place. It's exactly where it should be.

On Friends, everyone had their own years when the entire world was talking about their character. Season one was David Schwimmer's; season two was Lisa; seasons five and six were Courteney and myself; Jen was seasons seven and eight, and Matt (Most Improved Friend) was seasons nine and ten. Some of them won Emmys for those seasons, and I believe all of us should have won more, but I believe there is a bias against gorgeous rich people with apartments that are far too large for reality in New York City... Except, as I was continuously saying, there was no fourth wall.

David showed up one day in my dressing room during that first year. He'd given his persona a unique hangdog expression, and he was hilarious. He was also the first of us to shoot a commercial, appear on The Tonight Show, buy a property, and star in his own film. That first year, he was undeniably the hot man. He'd been amusing.

He sat opposite me in my dressing room that day and began talking.

"Matty," he explained, "I've been thinking." When it comes to contract renegotiation, we should work as a group. "We should all be paid the same." He was by far the best positioned to negotiate. I couldn't believe what he said. Needless to say, I was ecstatic. I was more than pleased to take advantage of his generous spirit.

It was a decision that proved to be tremendously profitable in the long run. David had every opportunity to make the maximum money, but he chose not to. I'd like to think I would have made the same decision, but as a greedy twenty-five-year-old, I'm not sure. But his decision forced us to look out for each other during what turned out to be a slew of difficult network negotiations, and it gave us enormous influence. We were generating a million dollars per episode by season eight, and even more by season 10. We were making $1,100,040 each episode and requesting fewer episodes. We're all idiots. We owed all we had been offered to David's goodness and strong economic judgement. David, I owe you approximately $30 million. (We were still a bunch of idiots.)

Being on Friends was one of those once-in-a-lifetime experiences in which the news just kept getting better and better. But things weren't going so smoothly off-screen. I went on Jay Leno in late April 1996 and confessed I was single. It had been too much for me to date Julia Roberts. I was convinced she was going to end her relationship with me—why wouldn't she? I was insufficient; I could never be sufficient; I was broken, bent, and unlovable. So, rather than go through the misery of losing her, I ended my relationship with the stunning and great Julia Roberts. She might have thought she was slumming it with a TV person, and now the TV guy was breaking up with her. I can't even begin to explain her puzzled expression.

I opted to party with the Murray brothers on Cape Cod. I'm not sure why I chose Cape Cod or why the Murray brothers joined me. I assumed it was just a new bar to try out. But it was then that I recognized something had changed—a new dynamic was at work. The days of anxiously approaching ladies with poor lines were past; girls were approaching me and talking to me. They approached me as I stood in a corner with a vodka tonic in my hand.

But none of them were Julia Roberts.

I've detoxed over 65 times in my life, the first time when I was twenty-six. My Vicodin habit had now become really problematic. If you watch Friends season three, I hope you're shocked at how thin I am at the end of the season (opioids mess with your appetite and make you puke all the time). In the last episode, you'll see that I'm wearing a white shirt and tan slacks, both of which appear to be at least three sizes too large for me. (Compare this to how I perceive the final episode of season six and the first episode of season seven—the Chandler-Monica proposal episodes. I'm wearing the same clothing in the sixth and seventh episodes [which are intended to air on the same night], but I must have lost fifty pounds in the off-season. During Friends years, my weight fluctuated between 128 and 225 pounds.)

You can follow the progression of my addiction by comparing my weight from season to season—when I'm overweight, it's drink; when I'm thin, it's medicine. I take a lot of medicines when I have a goatee.

By the end of season three, I was spending the majority of my time finding out how to get fifty-five Vicodin each day—I had to have fifty-five every day or I'd become sick. Making calls, seeing doctors, faking migraines, and locating corrupt nurses who would give me what I needed was a full-time job.

It had taken me some time to comprehend what was going on. I'd been taking about twelve pills a day at first, then went cold turkey one day and felt terrible. Something is seriously wrong with me, I thought, yet I persisted. I'll finish the season of Friends before getting therapy for this.

That decision almost cost me my life. I wouldn't be here if the season had lasted another month.

I was never stoned while working. I adored those people and wanted to always be there for them while playing second base for the New York Yankees. But addiction wakes up before you do, and it wants nothing to do with you. Alcoholism will always triumph. When you raise your hand and say, "I'm having a problem," alcohol sneers, "Are you going to say anything about it?" Okay, I'll leave for a time. But I will return.

It never truly goes away.

I swiftly booked another film, Almost Heroes, a comedy directed by Christopher Guest and starring Chris Farley. For that, they paid me $2 million. We shot it in a slum area of Northern California, near Eureka. Farley was as amusing as you'd expect, though his addictions, along with mine, meant that we barely made it through the stupid thing. I was exhausted from shooting Friends and Almost Heroes at the same time. The medicines weren't working as they used to. To avoid feeling sick all the time, I had to take a particular quantity of pills.

Eating also interfered with the high, so I never ate. In addition, I was always so nauseous that I didn't want to eat. I couldn't stop vomiting. This was good in private, but not so much in the middle of the woods with Christopher Guest. You're going to puke in thirty seconds. You'd better find a way to excuse yourself quickly. I puked behind trees, behind rocks, and in ladies' restrooms. I'd heard of individuals rummaging through their own vomit for pill bits to re-administer, but I couldn't bring myself to do it. I already had so many doctors on staff that I was rarely in that situation. But I did keep two towels by my toilet, one to wipe away the vomit and the other to wipe away the tears. I knew I was dying, but I couldn't tell anyone.

Then Chris Farley passed away. His sickness had advanced faster than mine. (Plus, I had a healthy horror of the word "heroin," which neither of us shared.) When I found out, I punched a hole in Jennifer Aniston's dressing room wall. Keanu Reeves is amongst us. I had to market Almost Heroes two weeks after he died, and I found myself publicly describing his drug and alcohol-related death.

I was stoned the entire time.

Nobody knew—not my family, not my friends, not anyone. I was quite ill all of the time. I'd attempt to quit every now and then—three days here, four days there—but it only made me unhappy and sick, and I couldn't do it.

I was at home one night, trying to make sense of everything, when an ex-girlfriend called.

"I know there is something wrong with you," she said. "I'm also taking you to the doctor."

I collapsed. Everything was shown to her. I'd never cried so hard in my life. The secret had been revealed. Someone else was aware.

The next day, I went to see a doctor. He directed me to Hazelden.

"They have a big lake there," the doctor added, and I reasoned that it was Minnesota, which was close enough to Canada. At the very least, I'll feel at ease amid the gloomy weather.

But I was terrified to death. This is happening now. I was on my way to rehabilitation. I was twenty-six at the time. I went to Hazelden to go off medications and learned absolutely nothing. The goal was for me to go through a quick detox before heading up to Minnesota. In a fast detox, you are sedated for two or three days and are given opiate antagonists. You're expected to be sober by the end of it. (By the way, I now know it doesn't work, despite the fact that it's still used as a treatment.) So I completed the quick detox and then headed up to Hazelden, but when I got there, I felt like I was dying. They say that opioid detoxes can't kill you, but they can make you wish you were dead. (Alcohol and benzos are the detoxes that can kill you.) I was in my Hazelden room, and I was extremely sick—I kicked like a fucking dog. Legs and arms quivering and jerking in dread. I was constantly pleading for help, only to be told, "You're detoxed, just relax."

But I hadn't detoxed—I'd simply gone from 55 Vicodins per day to zero Vicodins per day, effectively cold turkey. I became a "wall hugger"—to take even a few feet, I had to grasp onto the nearest wall. I know now that if I hadn't done the rapid detox, I would have been given something to relieve the pain, but they assumed I'd detoxed and left me alone. I suppose going from fifty-five to nothing indicates I was a fucking strong person, but it was the purest kind of agony. I was in a group session about ten days into my stay when everything started to blur. I was told that I kept saying, "I'm fine, totally fine," but I wasn't. My early conditioning—that I could never be a bad boy—was so powerful that I had to make sure I didn't rock the boat even when experiencing a grand mal seizure.

When I awoke from the seizure, I was back in my room, and the entire staff was horrified. "Oh my God, I can't believe you guys came to California to see me," I responded, not comprehending what had transpired and clearly still puzzled. That's wonderful!"

"You're not in California," someone pointed out; "you're in Minnesota." You experienced a grand mal seizure."

I stayed for another two weeks, and by the end, I felt like I ran the place, like I was the king. And I did it by merely imitating Michael Keaton in Clean and Sober. I was still young enough to gain some weight, play a lot of tennis, and stop taking medicines. But I knew deep down that I was going to drink again. I returned to California after I was better—I wasn't back to normal yet, but I was alright. But, as I previously stated, I had learnt nothing about what was wrong with me. I hadn't learned about AA or how to live a clean life; I'd simply stopped taking Vicodin. For those of you who were watching, this was the start of season four, and it was the best I ever watched on the program. Still not good enough for Jennifer Aniston, but damn close. Back in California, I endured 68 days before having my first drink, believing that it wasn't the thing that had nearly killed me. Opioids nearly killed me; vodka had only ever filled the holes, and since the holes remained, something had to fill them.

Until 2001, I drank every night. The run-up to Hazelden had been probably the best year of my life, the best year anyone could ever wish for. The joys of fame had not quite worn off, though if I'd died then, my headstone would have read either: HERE LIES MATTHEW PERRY—HE BROKE UP WITH JULIA ROBERTS or, COULD I BE MORE STUPID AND DEAD?

In 1999, I fell hard for a woman I was working with on a movie. (I was starting to have a track record of falling for women who were famous, just as my mother had been in Canada.) All the walls dropped, and I was just myself … and then she picked somebody else to be in love with.

I've been able to get most people I've wanted, but this one still hurts. Which just shows that the exception proves the rule: when I can get someone, I have to leave them before they leave me, because I'm not enough and I'm about to be found out, but when someone I want doesn't choose me, that just proves I'm not enough and I've been found out. Heads they win, tails I lose. Either way, to this day if someone mentions her name, my stomach clenches. The fear that drives my every waking minute has come true. She had even mentioned that my drinking was a problem—just another thing that addiction has cost me. You would think that might knock somebody sober, but it actually made it worse. I lit candles all over my house, drank, watched the movie we were in together, torturing myself, alone, heartsick, trying to get over it. Failing.

It was risky because I was swollen and looked bad. When I was in ninth grade in Ottawa, I realised Michael J. Fox had both the number one movie and the number one TV show at the same time, and even at fourteen, steam came out of my ears with jealousy. "You want the attention, the money, and the best seat in the house," I later told The New York Times. Fast forward to the hiatus between Friends seasons five and six, and I found myself filming The Whole Nine Yards, and when it came out in early 2000, I had the number one TV program and the number one movie. Me? I couldn't leave my room since I was taking so many medicines. So, at a time when Matthew Perry should have been rejoicing and being the top of the town, I was dealing with drug dealers and living in dark rooms and despair. When a penguin gets hurt in the wild, the other penguins gather around it and prop it up until it recovers. This is what my Friends coworkers did for me. When I was really hungover on set, Jen and Courteney, who believe in cardio as a cure-all, had a Lifecycle exercise bike put backstage. I'd go back there in between rehearsals and take and ride that thing like the fires of hell were after me—anything to restore my brain power back to normal. I was the injured penguin, but I was determined not to disappoint these beautiful folks or this spectacle.

But the addiction still plagued me—once, in a scene in the café while dressed in a suit, I fell asleep right on the couch, and tragedy was averted only when Matt LeBlanc prodded me awake immediately before my line; no one noticed, but I knew how close I'd come.

But I was always there, and I always had the lines. Then I had pancreatitis. I was thirty years old at the time. It was during the break. I was alone once more, and nothing was happening—no movie to film, nothing, just slow, tar-like time seeping down the LA canyons toward the unending sea. I was basically staying at home for months drinking—alone so I could drink; alone because I was drinking. (As I have stated, alcoholism is frantic to get you out on your own.) I was watching Meet Joe Black on repeat, despite the fact that it's about the character Death (me) attempting to discover what love is. Perfect. But it was as if I were Joe Black, being asked again and over, "What do we do now?" I was like death—I'd drink, watch the movie, pass out, wake up, drink, watch the movie again, and pass out again.

Then, almost out of nowhere, I felt a knife go into my stomach. It entered the membrane, twisted slightly, and caught on the veins, heating my blood to boiling and beyond. As the knife sank deeper and deeper, I could hear myself howling in agony, like an animal being ripped to bits in the canyons.

I called Jamie Tarses, my sort-of girlfriend at the time, and managed to explain, "There's something wrong."

Jamie was a God-sent angel who came right over to my house, loaded me into a car, and took me to the nearest hospital.

"You gotta pump my stomach!" I screamed in the ER. You have to pump my stomach!"

The doctor just stood there staring at me.

"I'm not going to pump your stomach. It is not due to food poisoning."

"Then, what the fuck is it?" I sobbed.

"You have pancreatitis," he informed her. "Which is something you can only get from drinking too much."

Pancreatitis can be caused by an inflammatory condition, an infection, or gallstones, but the most common cause is excessive alcohol consumption. Pancreatitis at thirty years old was unheard of. Good for me! Another milestone.

"Fuck that," I exclaimed. I don't drink excessively..." It could have been embarrassment or denial. I believe they are difficult to distinguish. Whatever it was, I insisted on Jamie driving me home.

After about an hour at my house, I realised something was still terribly wrong, so we proceeded to a different hospital, but received the same response. I was in the hospital for thirty days and nights, being fed fluids through an IV (the only way to treat pancreatitis was to leave the pancreas completely alone, which meant I couldn't eat or drink anything for about thirty days); and every one of those nights, I'd fall asleep with Jamie Tarses by my side—she had a bed moved in, the whole shebang—and I'd wake up to find her there, too. (I still feel Jamie was a kind God's emissary, and that none of us were worthy of her—I certainly wasn't.) While I smoked in my hospital room, we'd watch The West Wing over and over. It was either a different era or I was so famous at the time that it didn't matter. At one point, they apprehended me and instructed me to halt. But since I was desperate, I checked myself out of the hospital, smoked, and then checked myself back in. Going through intake again took seven hours. It was well worth it.

They hooked me up to a machine that gave me regular doses of a pain reliever called Dilaudid. If only it arrived in human form, it is an opioid that modifies the brain's connection to pain. But Dilaudid was my new favourite medicine, and I could have stayed in that hospital for a hundred days if they had kept giving it to me. I had Jamie by my side for thirty days, and I was high and joyful. I was very thrilled when I signed the deal for seasons six and seven, which brought us $50 million thanks to David Schwimmer's unselfish and great initiative. With a feeding tube in my arm and Dilaudid coursing through my veins, I signed the contract. They were on to me, though, because I was definitely asking for too much of the wonder medicine.

"You're fine," one doctor assured her. "Your pancreatitis has ended. You must return home. Tomorrow."

"You mean you're not going to give me Dilaudid tonight?"

"No," he replied, "we are not."

I survived the night, but no one knew what to do with me.

My father takes the stage on the left. He offered to have me live with him and his family in Ojai, a town northwest of Los Angeles.

"Come live with us," he invited, "and attend some AA meetings." "Get your facts straight."

It was an acceptable choice, and as I had nothing better to do, I returned to my home on Chelan Way in the Hollywood Hills to pick up some items. I was sober, but I'd only been on Dilaudid for thirty days, so I was still a little loopy. Jamie waited while I packed a bag, and then I followed her in my green Porsche out through the Hills' winding roads. As I turned left onto Chelan Drive, there was a courier van coming straight at me, so I swerved and pumped the brakes, but the car hit some grass and just kept going, and I drove into the stairs leading up to a house, demolishing them, and then into the living room. Fortunately, no one was home, but the car and stairs were totaled.

Once again, fucking stairwells. I did the proper thing and waited for the cops. I kept looking up at the sky, waiting for the next cartoon anvil to fall on my head. I was there long enough for someone to photograph me and sell it to People magazine—my car was parked in a house, and I was on my way to visit my father in Ojai.

It seemed like I was fifteen again, living in California with my father. Every day, a car would arrive to pick me up and drive me to the Friends set. But it wasn't long before I picked up Vicodin again, and then I started drinking and liked it again. "Reality is an acquired taste," my therapist said, and I had failed to acquire it. I was sneaking drugs and alcohol into my father's house, and his wife was so upset that my father approached me gently and informed me that I had to leave. Oh, I'll leave, but neither of you will ever see a dollar of my money, I thought, but I didn't say anything.

Everyone realised that something had to be done when I returned as a kite for the next season of Friends high. I'd already heard about methadone, a medicine that claimed to be able to kick a fifty-five-a-day Vicodin addict in one day with just one sip. The only catch was that you had to drink that little taste every day or go into severe withdrawal. My frantic mind thought, "Sounds good to me." I took the medicine right away and was ready to go back to Friends the next day. Methadone was said to have no adverse effects. This was not the case. It was, in reality, the beginning of the end. Everything else was going swimmingly. Friends was still as popular as ever. Then another cast member arrived at my trailer. It wasn't David this time, and the news wasn't good.

"I know you're drinking," she pointed out.

I'd long since gotten over her—I'd been fine since she started dating Brad Pitt—and had figured out how long I could look at her without feeling embarrassed, but being confronted with Jennifer Aniston was terrible. And I was perplexed.

"How can you tell?" I wondered. I never worked while inebriated. "I've been attempting to conceal it..."

"We can smell it," she murmured in a strange but loving tone, as the plural "we" slammed into me like a sledgehammer.

"I know I'm drinking too much," I admitted, "but I'm not sure what to do about it."

When I wasn't feeling well enough to drive to the set (I never worked high, but I certainly worked hungover), I'd hire a limo—that will get you some strange stares, let me tell you. Everyone would ask if I was okay, but no one wanted to stop the Friends train since it was so profitable, and I felt terrible about it. My greatest joy was also my greatest fear—I was so close to ruining this lovely thing. I eventually found a sober coworker, but it wasn't really helpful. I had taken some kind of drug and had drunk the night before, and it all came together during a run-through in front of everyone one day. But there was a strange twist to this one: I was hammered but didn't realise it, so I assumed I had nothing to hide. I had no idea I was drunk, yet I was slurring. People couldn't understand a single word I said. However, I had no idea. When I returned to my dressing room, everyone from the show was there.

"What are you going to do, Matty?" they wondered.

"It's medication; I'll take care of it." I apologise."

I didn't drink that night and went to work the next day, but I was on thin ice. I dialled my boss's number.

"They're on you," he said.

The authors, the performers, everyone knew, so I told them, "You've got to get me a movie." At the moment. "Please get me out of here."

My plan was to pull another geography. I still believed that if I distanced myself from the circumstances, I would be able to stop using drugs and drinking and come out fighting. (All I was doing was double my workload while the drinking and drug use escalated.) Because you are everywhere you go. This reminded me of the day I pleaded for a pilot and ended up with L.A.X. 2194. I'd had enough juice back then to get a pilot and thus enough money to drink at the Formosa; now, as the new century dawned, I had enough juice to get a movie if I wanted it. Serving Sara would be filmed in Dallas, and I had no idea why I felt that would be the ideal location for a sober lifestyle....

Serving Sara was a lousy film, but it was made even worse by my performance in it. I was in bad shape and had overextended myself. I was working on the film four days a week and then going back to Los Angeles on a private plane to do Friends. I'd have a water bottle filled with vodka on the plane that I'd sip from as I went over my lines. (In fact, if you're keeping track, I was on methadone, Xanax, cocaine, and a full quart of vodka every day.) When I arrived in Dallas for a scene, I realised we'd already shot it a few days before. Things were starting to fall apart.

Jamie Tarses travelled out to Texas and became my nurse, but I was still drinking and taking drugs and attempting to hide it from her. We were watching TV one night when she turned to me and said, "It looks like you're disappearing."

A window cracked open, yet it was open.

"I don't want to disappear," I said quietly. "Stop doing everything."

I called my manager, my father, and everyone else.

"I'm completely fucked-up," I admitted. "I require assistance. "I should go to rehab."

Serving Sara was closed down, which cost me $650,000. It was a small amount to pay to preserve my life. Friends rescheduled my scenes. And off I went to a detox centre in Marina del Rey, on the westside of Los Angeles. I was a car going 200 kilometres per hour that had just collided with a brick wall; a green Porsche colliding with a stairway. (Stairwells, fucking stairwells.)

"Go to your room; you're not taking any more drugs," they stated the first day, but they might as well have added, "Go to your room and just don't breathe anymore."

"But I have to breathe in order to live."

"No. It's been done before. People have stopped breathing there."

That's exactly how it felt. I stayed for a month. During my visit, I was smoking a cigarette while it was pouring and a light bulb was swinging in the smoking section. "This is what hell is," I exclaimed. "I'm stuck in hell."

I finally picked up the Big Book of Alcoholics Anonymous in Del Rey. I read somewhere around thirty pages in, "These men were not drinking to escape; they were drinking to overcome a craving beyond their mental control."

I put down the book and began to cry. I'm crying just thinking about it. I wasn't the only one. There were a large number of folks who shared my viewpoint. (This line was penned by William Silkworth on July 27, 1938.) It was an incredible and terrifying moment all at the same time. This statement indicated that I will never be alone again. It also meant that I was an alcoholic who would have to stop drinking and drugging right now and every day for the rest of my life, one day at a time.

"This guy is hard-core," Marina del Rey residents claimed. Thirty days will not suffice for him. He needs long-term care." So they transferred me to a Malibu recovery facility, where I spent the first twelve days not sleeping at all. My liver enzymes were skyrocketing. But after approximately three months, I began to improve—I participated in the groups and "did the work," as they say. When

Monica and Chandler married, I was in recovery. It was the 17th of May, 2001.

I'd been detoxing for two months when the powers that be decided to give us all the night off to watch the Academy Awards on March 25, 2001. "The nominees for best performance by an actress in a leading role are: Joan Allen, in The Contender; Juliette Binoche, in Chocolat; Ellen Burstyn, in Requiem for a Dream; Laura Linney, in You Can Count on Me; and Julia Roberts, in Erin Brockovich," Kevin Spacey announced from the podium.

"And the Oscar goes to... Julia Roberts!" he added.

I watched as Julia kissed her then-boyfriend, actor Benjamin Bratt, and proceeded up the steps to accept her award.

"Thank you, thank you, ever so much," she exclaimed. "I'm overjoyed..." As she spoke, a voice rose in that rehab room, frantic, sorrowful, tender, angry, imploring, full of longing and tears, battling with the universe while God calmly tapped his cane on the harsh, cold world.

I cracked a joke.

"I'll take you back," I assured her. "I'll take you back."

The entire group laughed, despite the fact that this was not a humorous line from a sitcom. This was now real life. Those individuals on TV weren't my people anymore. No, the folks I was lying in front of, trembling and wrapped in blankets, were now my people. And I was fortunate to have them. They were attempting to save my life.

I climbed into bed and stared at the ceiling on Julia's big night in Hollywood. That night, I wouldn't be able to sleep. Just thoughts flying through my head like a bullet discharged into a tin can. That blue truck, and that mountain peak. All the blue vehicles, all the mountaintops, disappeared like ether in a terror vacuum. I was quite thrilled for her. As for me, I was simply grateful to have survived another day. The days are long when you're at the bottom.

I didn't need an Oscar; all I wanted was one more day.

CHAPTER 5

Bruce Willis

I was feeling better after three months of therapy.

I was really happy to be back on my feet and live a life that was not completely dictated by my booze and addiction. I had stopped drinking and doing drugs. And my desire for each had vanished. Something much, much bigger than me was suddenly in charge. Miracles do occur.

The first thing I did was drive to Jamie Tarses' residence.

"I need time to process being sober," I told her, "and that will take up all of my time." I'm eternally grateful for what you've done for me."

I could see the colour fading from her face.

"But ... "Right now, I can't be in a relationship," I explained.

To be clear, I ended our relationship in order to fully compensate beautiful, wonderful Jamie for two years of giving up big sections of her own very busy and important life by essentially becoming my nurse. Jamie Tarses was one of the most wonderful, attractive, and intelligent people I'd ever met. I admired how her intellect functioned. And I ended things with her. Proving that getting sober didn't make me smarter—in fact, it may have made me a complete moron. Jamie was the most incredible person I'd ever met, and she adored me. But I wasn't prepared for it.

Of course, everything I said to Jamie that day was nonsense. I was recently sober, a huge celebrity, and I wanted to sleep with every single girl in Southern California.

And so I did. [Insert cartoon anvil crashing down on my head here.]

I had no trouble landing dates because of my celebrity. And this is how I opened every single one of them.

"Hello, I apologise for being late.

"By the way, you look fantastic. I've been looking forward to finally meeting you." [Pause to allow for an adequate favourable answer.]

"But I don't want to get off on the wrong foot here," I'd say. "I want to be as open as possible." I'm a walking open book. If you ask me anything, I'll tell you the truth."

More warmth would be shared here; on a good day, she would be nodding along, adoring my transparency, emotional tone, and suave involvement. Then I'd lower the hammer.

"I'm not sure what you're looking for, but if it's an emotional connection, I'm not your man." [Pause to take it all in.]

"I'm not going to call you every day," I said further, "and I'm not going to be your boyfriend." But if you're searching for a good time, I'm your man."

As it turned out, the great twentieth-century philosopher Cyndi Lauper was correct—girls simply want to have fun. But just in case the message wasn't obvious enough, I added some salt to the hearty stew I was serving.

"I'm an extremely passionate person," I admitted, slightly embarrassed, in case they thought I was protesting too much. "In fact, I'm a sucker for love. Even while I'm pounding the elliptical machine, all I can think about is songs about women under duress.

"But I am not looking for, or available for, any kind of emotional relationship," I said again, just in case the message was a little hazy. "I just got out of a long-term relationship and got sober, and I'm not looking to get back into one."

It was then time to perfect the landing.

"Oh, did you want to take a look at your menu?" I'd say. "I've heard that the food here is fantastic."

After all of that, it's astounding how many ladies joined up for this. Many of them, I'm sure, thought they could change me. What do you mean? Of course, there was the occasional abrupt walkout. A few ladies would remark, "Well, I'm not interested in that at all," and walk away. (It's no surprise that those were the ones I was most interested in.)

But, for the most part, my speech went off without a hitch. I use the term "worked" quite loosely. Because it goes without saying that the best you could say about all of this is that you could swap my head for a donkey's ass and no one would notice. Not only had I just broken up with the most beautiful lady on the planet, but what I was proposing was a complete waste of time. Sex is fine and all, but I believe I would be a much happier person now if I had spent those years looking for anything more.

This may have been my biggest blunder in a life full of them. And mistakes are difficult to reverse. During that time, I met at least five ladies with whom I could have married and raised children. If I'd only done it once, I wouldn't be sitting in a huge house overlooking the beach with no one to share it with except a sober friend, a nurse, and a gardener twice a week—a gardener I'd frequently go outside and give a hundred dollars to so he'd turn off his fucking leaf blower. (How come we can send a man on the moon but not create a silent one?)

One of these women was Natasha Wagner. She's not only gorgeous, brilliant, kind, and sensual; she's also the daughter of Natalie Wood and Richard Gregson (and was raised by Robert Wagner and Jill St. John after her mother's terrible death). Natasha had everything; she was flawless! But I wasn't aiming for perfection; I wanted more. Much more, much more. So, because I'd given her the speech and then failed to date her properly, we split up, and I was left to find even more beautiful women when I'd already found them.

A few years later, I was driving down the Pacific Coast Highway in some type of fuck-off-everyone automobile, a car so fantastic that I can't remember what make it was. The top was down, and the gleaming sun was plucking at the edges of the surf out in the water, turning it into a slippery silver. Dudes on surfboards sat around waiting for The One, who never arrived; I knew precisely how they felt. My phone then rang. Natasha was the one. She'd fallen for me after one of these dates, so she'd had to leave—that's the rule, Matty, that's the rule!—but she was still a friend, even if I'd dumped her.

"Hey, Matty!" she exclaimed, her face beaming. She was always as bright as the sun on the sea. I had to glance away from time to time just to regain my bearings.

"Hello, Natasha!" "How are you doing?" I said. It was wonderful to hear from her. "What's going on with you?"

Maybe if she called, there was a chance we could...?

"I'm a mother!" she said. "I recently gave birth to a baby girl." Clover!"

"Oh...," I said, then soon recovered, or so I thought. "That's wonderful news, honey. "I adore that name as well!"

We talked for a few minutes longer before hanging up the phone. Then, out of nowhere, the fuckyou-everybody car pulled over—because I was pulling it over—and I lurched to a stop on the shoulder. The sun was still shining brightly, and the surfers were up on their boards, but I was overcome with emotion. In my head, the massive wave that everyone was looking for was happening.

"She could have had that child with me," I told no one, sobbing like a baby.

I was depressed and lonely. I cried for approximately 45 minutes before a new idea came to me, like clouds spanning the sky above an ocean: Jesus, this is quite a reaction.... It was up to me to figure out why I'd broken down so badly. I sat there, thinking and wondering, until I realised what I'd been doing: I'd been hunting for an hour or two of pleasure with every woman ever invented when there was so much life I was missing. Is this why I became sober? To have sex with women? Surely, God had something greater in mind for me. I'd have to find out quickly. Natasha's life was flowering, whilst mine was spiralling out of control.

When I try to figure out how sobriety and addiction work for me, I keep going back to this line: Unless anything happens, I'm capable of being sober. On quiet days while I was sober, I'd reflect on the recent past and wonder why I'd ever relapsed after becoming clean. When I was sober, strong, and feeling like a normal person, I'd fantasise about donning a baseball cap and sunglasses and wandering around the La Brea Tar Pits or standing next to a celebrity's star on the Walk of Fame, just to see what it was like. Not in the sense of "I'm a star, I'm better than them"; rather, "Oh, so this is what a sober life feels like."

But even in sobriety, I was frequently just a tourist. It was quite difficult to establish roots in it. Why was it so difficult for me when I'd watched hundreds of others do it with impunity? I was dating everyone and anybody in LA, but I'd found a woman I genuinely adored in New York. I wasn't faithful to her, but I loved her anyway. I was newly sober and renowned, and I wanted to fuck everyone in Los Angeles County; many agreed. My speech was far more effective than it had any right to be. But the woman I fell in love with in New York was like a nice mother—a fantastic caretaker and so gorgeous that of course I was drawn to her and, of course, I messed it up. But it wasn't all bad—in LA, I was also working to assist other alcoholics become sober—sponsoring individuals, answering phone calls when necessary, and giving counsel. Friends was also a juggernaut, and I didn't have to worry about screwing that up because I was clean and ready to have my season, the one where everyone was talking about Chandler. (I was fully sober for the entire Friends season in 1989. Do you want to guess which year I was nominated for an Emmy for outstanding actor in a comedy? Season nine, indeed. Nothing will tell you anything if that doesn't. What was it that I did differently that season? I paid attention. I didn't simply stand there waiting for my turn to speak. Listening is sometimes more powerful than speaking. I've attempted to incorporate it into my daily life as well. Learn more and talk less. That has been my new slogan.) The two years went by; perhaps this is how most people feel. Perhaps I'd found my purpose; beyond Friends, beyond Hollywood, beyond everything, I was here to help people get and remain sober. Then something happened, and I'm capable of being sober unless anything else happens. One of the women I'd given the speech to had grown connected to me, and as we all know, if that occurs, I have to back down. That's exactly what I did. "I don't love you," I said. I warned you when I first met you.... Remember when I asked you about the menu during your speech?"

However, it was too late. It was my fault that she had an agony-hook in her. Is this why I became sober? To have sex with women? Then you hurt them? Surely, God had something greater in mind for me. I went to see her at the Beverly Hills Hotel at the time, but she could not be consoled. She reminded me of my mother—no matter how much charm I used, no matter how amusing I said, I couldn't make her feel better. She eventually rushed out of the room, leaving me alone in the room. A bottle of Vicodin was knocked over on the side table. Three pills had poured out in the light of the bedside lamp. I couldn't handle the situation because she was confined in the bathroom and screaming. This was anything that was going on. So I took three of the pills and got through the night, but it was the end of two years of abstinence.

I was in deep, deep shit once more. Because once you pierce the sobriety membrane, the phenomena of yearning kicks in, and you're off to the races once more. It was not possible for me to return. I swiftly progressed to buying my own medicines. Then I started drinking again. I was purposefully sliding down a lengthy slide into oblivion. But it was bigger than me, and there was nothing I could do about it. In retrospect, all I would have needed to do was tell someone about it, but that would have required me to quit. But halting was out of the question.

In 1999, I was sitting alone in my way-too-large mansion at the top of Carla Ridge, yet another house with a stunning view of the Los Angeles Basin. Normal Los Angeles life was going on someplace down there (Tar Pits; Walk of Fame)—up here, I was just waiting it out—drink in one hand, a continuous flow of Marlboro Lights in the other. Friends was five seasons in; Ross and Rachel had just stumbled out of a church wedded, ahead of Chandler and Monica. Friends was a cultural landmark, a millennium's shorthand, the world's number one show, and everyone's favourite show to watch. And that tone of voice! "Could this be any hotter?" had swept the country, and suddenly everyone was saying it. Clinton was in the White House; September 11th meant nothing unless it was your birthday or wedding anniversary. The entire world's water was running downward into a dazzling lake, in which the most beautiful, unnamed birds floated indefinitely.

A messenger had arrived at my door, breaking my meditation. It was as if I were reenacting what had happened to the Romantic poet Coleridge, who had been interrupted from his own high—he got his from opium—by the fabled "person from Porlock." Coleridge had memorised the entirety of his poem "Kubla Khan" at the time, but the messenger who had arrived at his door that day in 1797 had broken that memory, leaving only fifty-four lines for posterity. I wasn't Coleridge, but the view and the vodka tonic and the sweet Marlboro burn had rendered me into a safe place, where I wasn't alone, where a beautiful wife and a gaggle of amazing kids were tumbling around in the playroom while Daddy had some quality time alone in his screening room. (Would you like to be lonely? In a screening room, see a movie by yourself.) At times like these, when the haze was thickest, I might fantasise my life wasn't riddled with holes, that the minefield that was my past had been metal-detected and turned into a benign and lovely safety.

But now my doorbell was ringing, killing my buzz, and because I didn't have a wife or children, I had to grudgingly answer it. The "person from Porlock" delivered me a package containing a script called The Whole Nine Yards. And on it, my manager had written, "Could be paid dirt."

It wasn't really "Kubla Khan," but I could see it was going to be big. I was never good at reading scripts. I used to get offers for millions of dollars to make movies and only make it through the first few pages. I'm embarrassed to disclose it now, given that I'm writing scripts myself and finding it difficult to get actors to respond. Perhaps they feel the same way I did: that amid a life of fun, fame, and money, reading a script, no matter how big the number attached, feels all too much like school. But the universe will teach you. I was too this and that to read a script all those years, but last year I wrote a screenplay for myself and was attempting to get it made until I discovered I was too old to play the part. Most fifty-three-year-olds have already worked their asses off, so I needed to hire a thirty-year-old. I couldn't believe how disrespectful the person I chose was for taking weeks and weeks to respond.

"Do I still have enough clout to make an independent film?" In frustration, I approached my manager, Doug.

"Not really," Doug responded.

But back in 1999, my "person from Porlock" had sent me a script with potential that even I could see, and that potential was that none other than Bruce Willis was connected.

There was no larger cinematic star at the turn of the century than Bruce Willis. Look Who's Talking and its sequel, the Die Hard franchise, Pulp Fiction.... Nobody was more successful back then. Not to mention a pleasant change from the seventy-two romantic comedies I'd just finished. Mitchell Kapner had created a humorous script that was full of twists and turns, and it was simple to read: usually a good sign. Best of all, Bruce Willis appeared in it, and I played the starring role. I'll show you a disappointed wannabe movie star if you show me an acclaimed and prosperous TV star.

What about pay dirt? You bet your bottom dollar. But before, there was a supper with the director and my costar's brother.

The next night, I went to Citrus on Melrose. This was the Hollywood restaurant back then: pricey, exclusive, jacket required, and a queue of paparazzi at the door clicking away wildly at everyone who arrived and went. That night, the comings and goings were myself; the film's director, Jonathan Lynn, a short round British man who'd filmed My Cousin Vinny and who happened to be Oliver Sacks's cousin; and one of the film's producers, Bruce's brother, David (David has the hair, Bruce has the chin).

I'd dressed up in the obligatory movie-star black suit for the dinner, and I'd arrived a minute or two late because that's what movie stars do. The meal was a success, even though no one touched their dish, as is customary in Hollywood. Jonathan was really brilliant and funny—he had that dry, British sense of humour where he'd say something obviously serious but with a grin in his eye, just enough to indicate that he was busting balls. David was attentive, entertaining, and intelligent; as for myself, I had already decided to do the film. Because the initial script did not include any physical comedy, I stated, "I think this would be a great opportunity for some physical comedy, and I'd be more than willing to fall down a flight of stairs and leap down some mountaintops to work with Bruce Willis."

Jonathan and David were relieved as they chuckled. The "dinner" was eventually over. "Well, you're our guy—we really want you to do this," Jonathan said. I leapt into my forest-green Porsche and squealed away, hands shook and cameras disregarded.

I'm going to be the lead in a Bruce Willis film, I thought as all the lights on Sunset turned green once more. Back at Carla Ridge, the moon had risen, lonely and sorrowful, casting an odd and awkward shadow across my perspective. I turned on the television, poured a vodka tonic, and waited. The stars were aligning once more; had Matthew Perry's meteoric climb just taken another enormous leap forward? This was my thought as I watched the stars rise in a clean, dark sky. I began to count them, despite knowing the myth that once you reach a hundred, you die. I came to a halt at 99, just in case. I received a message on my answering machine the next morning.

"This is Bruce Willis, Matthew." Call me back, or I'll burn down your house, shatter both your knees and arms, and leave you with just stubs for hands and feet for the rest of your life."

Dial tone, click. I reasoned that this was a call I should return. We met a few days later at Ago, yet another posh Italian restaurant in Hollywood, in the private room in the back reserved for those of Mr. Willis's stature. I sped up in my Porsche, barely putting it in park long enough to pass the keys to the valet. But I was on time this evening. Bruce Willis did not disappoint—he exuded A-list glamour. He didn't simply take over a room; he became the room. In fact, I realised he was a real movie star when he showed the bartender how to prepare the ideal vodka tonic.

"Three-second pour," he instructed the terrified gentleman.

Bruce was forty-four years old, unmarried (he was divorced from Demi Moore at the time I met him), and he knew exactly how to make the ideal cocktail. He was at a party, and being near him was energising. After a while, Joe Pesci, whom Jonathan Lynn had directed in My Cousin Vinny, and several very lovely women paid us a visit in our own little room. Bruce chuckled at all my stupid jokes—he appeared to love the spectacle of a younger, funnier guy showing him respect and keeping up with his drinking (if only he knew). I was delighted to be in his company since he knew how to enjoy life. With their dinner undisturbed, the two new best friends went to his enormous mansion off Mulholland—Bruce, too, appeared to like a good view. The night culminated with Bruce Willis and Matthew Perry shooting golf balls into the San Fernando Valley below, cocktails in hand.

Those balls are going to land someplace, I reasoned, and before I could consider the damage a well-addressed five iron could do, or even the metaphorical nature of what we were doing, I had another drink.

"Welcome to the pros," Bruce said at one point, presumably referring to the life of a movie star rather than my golf skills. We'd started a friendship in which we drank together, made each other laugh, and complemented each other on our swings.

The dawn eventually came up, as it always does, and we said our blurry goodbyes. I recall thinking as I drove home, "Watch this guy—this is how to be happy." Nothing appeared to upset Bruce, and no one refused him. This was the A-leagues, after all. That same day, Bruce called to invite me back to his place for a screening of his upcoming film, but I was far too sick and hungover to even consider going. I excused myself and asked him what the movie was called so I could see it later.

"The Sixth Sense," he mentioned.

So, I'd obtained The Whole Nine Yards and formed a friendship with the world's most famous movie star, but I realised I was drinking way too much to pull off this movie. Extreme measures would be required. Some people could party all night and still show up for work—but they weren't addicted like me. If I wasn't going to go back to my hotel room and keep drinking, I'd need something else to wind down and make sure I could get to set the next day. I dialled the number of a friend—I use the term loosely—who I knew dealt Xanax.

"How many would you like to purchase?" he said.

"Give me a hundred," I requested.

I sat on my bed, counting them as they arrived. This way, I can drink with Bruce and the others, but when I'm finally alone, I can pop one of these and fall asleep. I was a man with a plan, but I was also ignoring the fact that this was a fatal mix. We travelled on Bruce's jet to Montreal to make The Whole Nine Yards, coming like conquering heroes ready to take over the town. I was the returned prodigal Canadian son, ready to party. We established ourselves in the Intercontinental Hotel. I had an ordinary room; Bruce had the entire top floor, which he instantly christened "Club Z," for no apparent reason. He also had a disco ball built within hours. The Globe

Restaurant quickly became our second home away from home. The money and drinks were flowing freely, and all of the waiters were glowing. I had started dating Renee a few months before. I met her at Red, a restaurant in Los Angeles. I was eating dinner with my pal Ben Weiss, the first assistant director of Friends, when our waiter walked up and sat next to me and began conversing with me. This did not appear to be typical waitress behaviour. After she took our order, I told Ben, "Her name is going to be Samantha."

"Nah," he replied, "she's definitely Jennifer."

"We're having a bet on your name," I replied as she returned with our food. I'm betting on Sam, and my pal says you're Jen."

"My name is Renee," she introduced herself. And then, after a few drunken parties, we were a couple. Renee had filled in for someone who had broken my heart in an earlier film, so she was already behind the eight ball... We were mostly on the outs by the time I traveled to Montreal, but in any case—and I'm not proud to say this—I would have fucked mud at that point in my life. That's Canadian mud.

The role itself was simple. All I had to do was pretend to be terrified of Bruce, which was simple, and pretend to be in love with Natasha Henstridge, which was even simpler. The director, Jonathan, whom I had nicknamed "Sammy" for some inexplicable reason, operated the type of set I enjoy—a very creative one. The funniest joke, regardless of origin, would be chosen, exactly like we did on Friends.

Amanda Peet also appeared in the film. She was humorous, smart, and very gorgeous, and even though she had a boyfriend, she didn't mind flirting, which she did with both Bruce and myself at the drop of a hat, to the point where Bruce yelled at her, "Pick one!"

Club Z was rocking at night because of Bruce's disco ball. Everyone still managed to arrive at work at 6:00 a.m. I say "somehow," but I know how I did it: those hundred Xanax worked like a charm, even if they did make my head seem like a Spalding basketball when paired with my drinking. Meanwhile, Mr. A-list Willis appeared to be opening an envelope with his chin. Every day, with me nursing a nasty hangover but still young enough to deal, we'd convene and look at the sides (TV and movie jargon for the day's work). "We" were me, Jonathan Lynn, Bruce Willis, and the funny Kevin Pollak, who played another crime leader, Janni Gogolak. It was almost like a writers' room—we'd talk about what may be humorous, what might belong here or there in a scene. A significant amount of effort was expended to include physical comedy for me to perform. I'd rush through windows and bang into doors. I once performed a take in which I spot a criminal, then turn, run into someone, get knocked back, crash into a lamp, pick up the lamp, and use it to protect myself from the baddie. Everything I came up with worked perfectly.

Kevin said at one point, "He shouldn't be able to breathe the air."

I advised him to include an excessively extended pause before the phrase "the air." Kevin's delivery of that line was so humorous, and the pause kept getting longer and longer with each take we did, that in the end he had to do his coverage with me in a different room. I only wanted to be Bruce Willis' pal after the veil was lifted. I didn't want to be like everyone else and be a suck-up to him. We had a three-day weekend while filming The Whole Nine Yards, and he flew Renee and me, as well as him and his girlfriend, to his house in Turks and Caicos. It's a lovely spot with a wonderful view of the ocean. They'd even considered purchasing all of the adjacent properties so that the paparazzi couldn't get their images. We took umbrellas with us all weekend to keep the sun off our faces and keep us from becoming too tanned for the movie. Mr. Willis taught me a new movie star trick, one of many.

But there was a significant difference between Bruce and myself. Bruce was a party animal, while I was a drug addict. Bruce has an on/off switch. He can party hard, then get a script like The Sixth Sense, quit partying, and nail the movie sober. He lacks the gene and is not an addict. There are many instances in Hollywood of people who can party and still function—I was not one of them. When I was drinking and using, if a cop came to my house and said, "If you drink tonight, you're going to jail tomorrow," I'd start packing for jail because once I start, I can't stop. All I could control was the first sip. All bets were off after that. (See also: The guy takes the booze, and the drink takes everything else.) I am no longer responsible for my behaviour once I believe the lie that I can only have one drink. I need individuals, treatment centres, hospitals, and nurses to assist me. I can't stop myself. And it was going to kill me if I didn't get a hold of it soon. I had a monster in my head, a monster that wanted to get me alone, get me to take that first drink or drug, and then consume me. Despite the partying, we were all pros on that film and produced a fantastic crowd pleaser. Early reviews were encouraging, with one saying, "Bruce Willis will deliver the customers, but it's Matthew Perry who will attract the most attention in a pratfall-filled turn that bears comparison to what Tom Hanks was doing 12-15 years ago."

This was excellent praise for someone who admired Tom. Bruce wasn't convinced the picture would work at all, and I'd bet him it would—if he lost, he'd have to do a guest appearance on Friends (he appears in three episodes of season six). For three weeks, The Whole Nine Yards was the number one movie in America.

I'd done it—the dream I'd had since ninth grade had finally come true: The Whole Nine Yards wasn't Back to the Future, but Michael J. Fox and I are the only two people who have had the number one movie and TV program at the same time.

I should have been the talk of the town, but back in Los Angeles, it was evident, at least to me, that my addiction had reached deadly proportions. I was almost unable to leave the house since drugs and drink had fully taken over. I was so high on drugs and dealing with drug dealers that I couldn't leave my room—rather than a grand moment of pure celebrity, dealing with dealers was all I could think about. Of course, I went to the movie premiere and turned on The Matthew Perry Show, but I was bloated and driven by fear of something I didn't comprehend.

I've always wanted to be on a talk show and be completely honest.

Jay Leno: How are you, Matthew?

Me: I have no idea which way is up. I'm completely screwed. I'm very depressed. I'm unable to get out of bed.This would have been an ideal time for it. Four years after The Whole Nine Yards, Bruce, Kevin, and I shot a sequel (this time with a different director). If The Whole Nine Yards was the beginning of my movie success, The Whole Ten Yards was the end.

We shot the second film in Los Angeles, and we were granted far too much leeway, which suffered. That's rare to recreate a good thing, and that was true here; the jokes were old, and the parties were even staler. In fact, it was so horrible that I later called my agents and said, "Am I still allowed to go to movies?"

When The Whole Nine Yards came out, I was so engulfed in addiction that I couldn't even leave my room. My messed-up psyche has been dragging my body down with it into a hellhole of despair and demoralisation. It recently occurred to me that this type of sensation should have been reserved for the release of The Whole Ten Yards. Anyone in their right mind would have been devastated by that one. At the end of the night, when the sun was just about to rise and everyone else had left, and the celebration had come to an end, Bruce and I would just sit and talk. That's when I saw the true Bruce Willis—a kind-hearted, caring, selfless man. A fantastic parent. And a fantastic actor. Most importantly, he's a nice guy. And if he wanted me to, I would be his lifelong friend. But, as with so many of these things, our paths never met again after that. Of course, I now pray for him every night.

CHAPTER 6

All Heaven Breaking Loose

"Dad," I continued solemnly, "I know this sounds crazy, but a giant snake is going to come and take me away at any moment."

What was my father's reaction?

"Matty, if a giant snake comes and takes you away, I will shit my pants." I'm still impressed by how my father handled my complete lunacy.

At this moment, the sober friend returned to the room and expressed his regret while still offering to assist me. But I needed to visit a doctor immediately. We set out to see him. I apologised to the doctor at the end of the consultation, shook his hand, and swore it would never happen again. And I meant it when I said I was done. The doctor prescribed new detox medications as well as anti-seizure medication (Xanax withdrawal can cause seizures). We returned home. Moira, my patient assistant, was summoned to pick up the prescription, and we waited. And then I waited. This new mission took her hours to complete for some reason.

But the clock was ticking. If I didn't obtain this detox medication soon, something bad was going to happen. I might have a seizure; I might die. Neither choice appealed to me. Three grown guys were now staring at the front door, waiting for it to open, and two of them were also staring at terrified Matty.

I couldn't take the scrutiny any longer and retreated to a small couch off to the side of the kitchen. Reality, that acquired taste, was gradually reasserting itself, like a lens focussing. And I was in excruciating pain, both literally and mentally. I was plagued by feelings of humiliation and remorse. I couldn't believe I'd done it yet again. The men I was sponsoring had a longer period of sobriety than I had. What you don't have, you can't give away. And I didn't have anything.

I despised myself. This was a new low; I didn't think you could go any lower than my prior low, but I had done it. And all of this happened in front of my horrified father. Addiction's crafty, perplexing, and overpowering nature had gotten the best of me yet again. The entrance door was still not opening. This was a major issue. I was in a bad situation. The narcotics were flowing freely, as was the alcohol. I couldn't even cry since things were so horrible. Crying may have indicated that there was some kind of normalcy around, but there was nothing natural about any of this.

So there you have it—the lowest point in my life. This is a classic moment for an addict, one in which they seek long-term therapy.... But wait, what's this? I noticed a crinkle in the air as I sat there looking into the kitchen. Someone who wasn't at their lowest point could have dismissed it as insignificant, but it was so intriguing to me that I couldn't turn away. It seemed like a small wave in the air. Nothing like it had ever happened to me before. It was genuine, authentic, palpable, and physical. Is this what you're looking at at the end? Was I going to die? And then… I began to pray wildly, with the desperation of a drowning man. I'd made a Faustian pact with a God who had merely drawn a deep breath and bided his damn time the last time I prayed, shortly before I'd acquired Friends. More than a decade later, I was testing my praying arm once more.

“God, please help me,” I whispered. “Show me that you are here. God, please help me.”

As I prayed, the little wave in the air transformed into a small, golden light. As I kneeled, the light slowly began to get bigger, and bigger, until it was so big that it encompassed the entire room. It was like I was standing in the sun. I had stepped on the surface of the sun. What was happening? And why was I starting to feel better? And why was I not terrified? The light engendered a feeling more perfect than the most perfect quantity of drugs I had ever taken. Feeling euphoric now, I did get scared and tried to shake it off. But there was no shaking this off. It was way way bigger than me. My only choice was to surrender to it, which was not hard, because it felt so good. The euphoria had begun at the top of my head and slowly seeped down throughout my entire body—I must have sat there for five, six, seven minutes, filled with it.

My blood hadn't been replaced with warm honey. I was warm honey. And for the first time in my life, I was in the presence of love and acceptance and filled with an overwhelming feeling that everything was going to be OK. I knew now that my prayer had been answered. I was in the presence of God. Bill Wilson, who created AA, was saved by a lightning-bolt-through-the-window experience where he felt he was meeting God.

This was mine.

But, feeling this good was terrifying. I was once asked if I'd ever been happy, and I almost bit that fucker's head off. (At Promises once, during a rehab, I'd told my counsellor that I was freaked-out by how happy everyone was recovering seemed. "They're like a bunch of happy people living on a hill while I'm dying," I'd said, and he'd explained to me that a lot of those people weren't getting it and didn't understand what was going on and would eventually be back in rehab and things would be even worse for them next time around.)

After about seven minutes (insert "seven minutes in heaven" joke here) the light began to dim. The euphoria died down. God had done his work and was off helping someone else now.

I started to cry. I mean, I really started to cry—that shoulder-shaking kind of uncontrollable weeping. I wasn't crying because I was sad. I was crying because for the first time in my life, I felt OK. I felt safe, taken care of. Decades of struggling with God, and wrestling with life, and sadness, all was being washed away, like a river of pain gone into oblivion.

I had been in the presence of God. I was certain of it. And this time I had prayed for the right thing: help.

Eventually the weeping subsided. But everything was different now. I could see colours differently, angles were of a different magnitude, the walls were stronger, the ceiling higher, the trees tapping on the windows more perfect than ever, their roots connected via the soil to the planet and back into me—one great connection created by an ever-loving God—and beyond, a sky, which had before been theoretically infinite was now unknowably endless. I was connected to the universe in a way I had never been. Even the plants in my house, which I had never even noticed before, seemed in sharp focus, more lovely than it was possible to be, more perfect, more alive.

I stayed sober for two years based solely on that moment. God had shown me a sliver of what life could be. He had saved me that day, and for all days, no matter what. He had turned me into a seeker, not only of sobriety, and truth, but also of him. He had opened a window, and closed it, as if to say, "Now go earn this."

Nowadays, when a particular darkness hits me, I find myself wondering if it was just Xanax insanity, a continuation of the snake I had been sure was about to show up—the drug can cause what the National Institutes of Health describe as "reversible brief psychotic episodes." (I later had a gigantic seizure in front of my father, too, which wasn't the most fun I've ever had—nor was being rushed to UCLA Medical Center, which at the time I thought was an angel way station.) But quickly I return to the truth of the golden light. When I am sober, I can still see it, remember what it did for me. Some might write it off as a near-death experience, but I was there, and it was God. And when I am connected, God shows me that it was real, little hints like when the sunlight hits the ocean and turns it into that beautiful golden colour. Or the reflection of sunlight on the green leaves of a tree, or when I see the light return to someone's eyes when they come out of the darkness into sobriety. And I feel it when I help someone get sober, the way it hits my heart when they say thank you. Because they don't know yet that I should really be thanking them.

A year later I met a woman I'd stay with for six years. God is everywhere—you just have to clear your channel, or you'll miss it.

CHAPTER 7

The Benefit of Friends

Monica was the first to go, and she placed her key on the vacant counter. Chandler was the next to leave. Then came Joey, who should not have had a key in the first place, followed by Ross, Rachel, and finally Phoebe. What do you say now that there are six keys on the countertop? We were all lined up in a lengthy queue. "I guess this is it," Phoebe replied, and Joey said, "Yeah," then almost broke the fourth wall by briefly glancing out at the audience before saying, "I guess so..."

But there was no fourth wall to break; there had never been one. We'd been in people's bedrooms and living rooms for a decade; in the end, we'd become such an important part of so many people's lives that we'd overlooked the fact that there had never been a fourth wall to break in the first place. We'd just been six close friends in an apartment that appeared to be much larger than it was, but was actually the size of a TV set in a living room.

Then it was time to say good-by to that apartment for the last time. There were now eight of us—the six main characters plus Monica and Chandler's twins in a stroller. I'd set Marta Kauffman aside before the final episode.

"Nobody else will care about this except me," I explained. "So, may I please have the last line?" That's why, when we all leave the apartment and Rachel suggests one more coffee, I get to close the curtain on Friends.

"Sure," Chandler said, before asking, for the final time, "Where?"

I adore the look on Schwimmer's face as I say that line—it's the right balance of affection and amusement, which is exactly what the program Friends has always provided to the globe. And that was the end of it. The truth was that we were all eager for Friends to end. For starters, Jennifer Aniston had decided she no longer wanted to do the show, and because we all made decisions as a group, we all had to stop. Jennifer wanted to do movies; I had been doing movies all that time and had The Whole Ten Yards, which was sure to be a hit (insert donkey's head now), but even though it had been the best job in the world, the stories of Monica, Chandler, Joey, Ross, Rachel, and Phoebe had all pretty much played out by 2004. It was not lost on me that Chandler had matured far faster than I had. As a result, ten was a brief season, mostly by Jenny's design. But by this point, all of the characters were fundamentally happy, and no one wants to see a bunch of happy people doing happy things—what's funny about that?

The date was January 23, 2004. The keys on the counter, a man who resembled Chandler Bing replied, "Where?," The song "Embryonic Journey" by Jefferson Airplane played as the camera panned to the rear of the apartment door, and Ben, our first AD and very close friend, exclaimed for the final time, "That's a wrap," and tears sprang from practically everyone's eyes like geysers. We'd made 237 episodes, including this one, suitably titled "The Last One." Aniston was sobbing, and I was surprised she had any water left in her body after a long time. Even Matt LeBlanc was in tears. But I didn't feel anything; I wasn't sure if it was due to the opioid buprenorphine I was taking, or if I was just dead inside. (For the record, buprenorphine is an amazing detox medication that is intended to help you stay off other "stronger" opiates—it does not modify you in any way. However, it is the most difficult drug in the world to quit. Bupe, also known as Suboxone, should never be used for more than seven days at a time. I had been on it for eight months because I was afraid of a bad detox.)

Instead of sobbing, I took a long walk around the stage with my then-girlfriend, Rachel, on stage 24 at Warner Bros. in Burbank (a stage that would be renamed "The Friends Stage" after the concert finished). We said our different goodbyes, promising to see each other soon in the way people do when they know it's not true, and then we walked out to my car.

For a little while, I sat in the parking lot and reflected about the previous ten years. I remembered L.A.X. 2194, the $22,500, and Craig Bierko; I remembered being the last one cast, and that trip to Vegas, when we could stroll through a crowded casino and no one knew who we were. I remembered all the gags and double takes, the Murray brothers, and some of my most famous/too-true lines, such as "Hi, I'm Chandler, I make jokes when I'm uncomfortable," and "Until I was twenty-five, I thought the only response to 'I love you' was 'Oh, crap!'" and "We swallow our emotions." Even if it means we'll be unhappy for the rest of our lives," and "Could she be more out of my league?"

I remembered the summer between seasons eight and nine, when I was in recovery and People magazine said on the cover that I was "Happy, Healthy, and HOT!" "Friends' funny guy talks about those dating rumours," the leader said, "the 'final' season, and his battle to get sober." 'It was terrifying,' he says. 'I didn't want to die,' she said. That summer, I had spent getting clean and playing a lot of tennis. I reflected on the first day of season four, following the summer in which I had gone to rehab in public. Obviously, everyone's attention was drawn to me at the initial table read. Kevin Bright, one of the show's executive producers, had started the conversation by asking, "Anyone want to chat about their summer vacations?" and I took advantage of the opportunity to break the ice by exclaiming, very loudly and solemnly, "OK! "I'll begin!" thus dispelling all tension in the room. Everyone applauded and laughed at me for turning my life around and showing up to work looking good and ready to work. It was perhaps the most brilliant joke I've ever told.

I remembered having to ask the producers to let me stop speaking like Chandler for the last several seasons (not to mention getting rid of those sweater vests). That specific cadence—could it be more annoying?—had become so ingrained that I thought I'd explode if I had to put the emphasis in the wrong place one more time, so I just went back to saying lines normally, for the most part in season six and beyond.

I remembered crying when I asked Monica to marry me. And, of course, there were negative thoughts. What will happen to me now that I don't have this crazy wonderful, creative job to go to every day? Friends had been a safe haven, a source of solace for me; they had given me a reason to get out of bed every morning, as well as a reason to take it a little easy the night before. We were having the time of our lives. It seemed like we got some wonderful news every day. Even I realised that only a madman (which I have been at times) could mess up a job like that.

As we drove home that night, I pointed out to Rachel a large billboard advertising The Whole Ten Yards. I was standing fifty feet tall, frowning in a dark suit and purple shirt and tie, next to Bruce Willis, who was dressed in a white T-shirt, pinafore, and bunny slippers. THEY MISSED EACH OTHER, it read in six-foot lettering above the tagline: WILLIS... PERRY. THEIR GOAL IS BETTER THIS TIME. I used to be a movie star. (Do you recall what I said about the donkey's head?)

My future, even without Friends, seems bright enough. I had a major film coming out; I'd done two episodes of Ally McBeal and three episodes of The West Wing, so I was gaining serious acting chops as well as humour (I'd received two Emmy nods for my three The West Wing appearances). I'd also recently wrapped The Ron Clark Story, a TNT film about a real-life small-town teacher who gets a job in one of Harlem's worst schools. There wasn't a single joke in the entire movie, which drove me insane, so off camera I developed a character named "Ron Dark" who was drunk and continually swore in front of the children. Despite this, it was a huge success when it finally broadcast in August 2006. I'd be nominated for a SAG award, a

Golden Globe award, and an Emmy. (I was defeated by Robert Duvall in all three. I couldn't believe I'd been beaten out by such a jerk.) But, as I previously stated, The Whole Ten Yards would be a flop—I doubt even my closest family and friends saw it. In fact, if you looked closely enough at the premiere, you could see people avoiding their gaze from the screen. I believe it has a 0 rating on Rotten Tomatoes. That was the moment Hollywood decided not to cast Mr. Perry in many more films. I had planned to attend a 12-step meeting the day following the final episode of Friends, with the intention of starting my new life on the right foot. But facing a blank canvas of an empty day was extremely difficult for me. I awoke the next morning wondering, "What the fuck am I going to do now?"

What the Hell could I possibly do? With no new work in sight, I was hooked on Bupe. Which was absurd given that I'd just concluded the most beloved show in television history. On top of that, my relationship with Rachel was deteriorating—physical distance was a problem, as was emotional closeness. I was damned if I did and damned if I did not. Then I was single once more. With no tremendously high-paying, dream-come-true job to go to and no special someone in my life, things deteriorated quickly—it seemed like I was going down a cliff. The lunacy of utilising additional, heavier substances seeped back into my twisted mind. It wasn't long before the seemingly unthinkable occurred once more. I began drinking and using.

Despite appearances, I was never suicidal, thank God—I never wanted to die. In truth, I always had a glimmer of optimism in the back of my mind. But, if dying was a result of being able to take the amount of medicines I required, then I would have to accept it. That's how distorted my thinking had become—I could hold those two thoughts in my head at the same time: I don't want to die, but if it's necessary to get enough narcotics on board, then amen to oblivion. I recall holding pills in my hand and thinking, "This could kill me," but taking them nevertheless.

This is a very narrow, and terrifying, line to walk. I had reached a point in my drinking and using where I had forgotten how much I was drinking and using. And it takes a nearly deadly degree of forgetfulness to achieve that level of amnesia.I was also hurting from loneliness; I could feel it in my bones. On the outside, I appeared to be the luckiest guy alive, so I could only complain to a few people without being ordered to shut up, and even then... nothing could fill the emptiness inside me. I once purchased yet another new car, the thrill of which lasted approximately five days. I moved frequently as well—the excitement of a new house with an even better view lasted slightly longer than the Porsche or Bentley, but not by much. I was also so introspective that having a true give-and-take relationship with a woman was nearly impossible; I was much better at friends with benefits, so whoever I was seeing didn't discover that insidious, creeping feeling that I was irredeemably not enough.

I was befuddled. There was nowhere else to go. I was everywhere I attempted to hide. Alcoholics despise two things: the status quo and change. I knew something had to change—I wasn't suicidal, but I was dying—but I was too afraid to act. I was a man in desperate need of a yellow light experience, so I will be eternally grateful that it happened in my house that day, because it gave me a new lease on life. I'd been given the gift of sobriety yet again. The only question was, what would I do with it? Nothing has ever worked in the long run. I'd have to change my approach to everything or I'd be toast. And I didn't want to be one of them. Not until I had learned to live and love. Not until the world began to make more sense to me.

My habit would have killed the wrong person if it had killed me. I wasn't totally myself yet; I was only parts of myself (and not always the nicest parts). My new way of life would have to begin with work, because it appeared to be the simplest place to begin. Accepting effort was my only hope. I got some sober time in and was able to get back on my feet. I also had a few friends-with-benefits relationships going on, one of which was gradually evolving into something more. Perhaps much more. I'd made friends with benefits before, but this? This was less evident to me. "Why don't you stick around and we can watch a movie?" I began to want her to stay past the sex. What was I up to? I was breaking every rule.

When we first met, she was twenty-three and I was thirty-six. In reality, I knew she was 23 since I had crashed her 23rd birthday party. Our first make-out session was in the backseat of a filthy Toyota (to think I'd spent all that money on nice automobiles and now I'm in the backseat of a tan Corolla). "I'm getting out of the car now," I said when we were finished. "It's mostly because I'm 36."

So began two years of potentially record-breaking sexual intercourse with no strings attached, both of us strictly adhering to the guidelines of friends-with-benefits. We were on the same wavelength. We never went out to eat or chatted about each other's families. We never talked about what was going on in each other's life with relation to other people. It was texting instead, with stuff like, "How about Thursday night at seven?"

She was harsh at first. I recall an early chat in which I informed her I was wearing a suit and thought I looked fairly decent.

"I hate suits," she admitted.

It took me years to break her out of her harshness. It's written somewhere in the actor's handbook—probably in the book my father gave me, the one he'd engraved with "another generation shot to hell"—that you had to try new things and expand yourself. If you've excelled in comedy, it's time to take a sharp right and become a tragic actor. As a result, that became the strategy. I couldn't retire, and a mature man could only spend so much time playing video games. "You live the life of someone who drinks and uses," my friends-with-benefits partner once stated to me, "you just don't drink and use." (Did I mention she was really intelligent?)

I was at a fork in the road. What do you do if you're an actor who is rich and famous but doesn't want to be rich and famous? You can either retire (you're far too young for that) or alter things up. I notified my management and agency that I was only seeking dramatic work at this time. It didn't seem like a wild move because I had dabbled in it with fantastic results on The West Wing, Ally McBeal, and The Ron Clark Story. I tried out for a few serious films but didn't get any of them. I shot a couple indie films that tried hard but didn't work out. Then a script came along that was red-hot. I'd never seen so much passion directed towards a project—it was magnetic. The sequel to their hit show The West Wing, Studio 60 on the Sunset Strip, was written by Aaron Sorkin and directed by Thomas Schlamme. They had almost fifteen Emmys between them, so their new endeavour created a frenzy in the fall of 2005 unlike anything before. I'd never seen a project with that much power behind it before it even began. To get that thing, NBC and CBS fought like gladiators, with NBC eventually winning out for something like $3 million per episode. Everywhere I looked that fall, someone was talking about Studio 7 on the Sunset Strip (its original name). I was wrapping up writing The Ron Clark Story in New York and staying at my favourite hotel in the world, the Greenwich in Tribeca. I was eager to read this fantastic script. I waited because the script would not arrive at my hotel until 10:00 p.m. because I was on the East Coast.

Aaron and Tommy had transformed the way Americans viewed serialised television with The West Wing, and I had changed the way Americans spoke English with Chandler Bing's cadences. It appeared to be a strong mix. I had read the script by 11:30 p.m. and chose to return to network television. The main characters were Matt Albie, the head writer of Studio 7 (a role that Aaron apparently wrote with me in mind), and Danny Tripp, his fellow showrunner, to be played by the kind and brilliant Bradley Whitford, both of whom were brought back to save an SNL-style show called Studio 60 on the Sunset Strip.

It had "giant, Emmy-winning hit" written all over it before a single frame was shot. It included Sorkin, Schlamme, and myself. What possibly could go wrong?

The first issue was money. I'd been making a huge nut on Friends and knew I'd struggle to obtain that figure again, but the fact that everyone in this ensemble production about a comedic TV show was being asked to accept the same fee blew me away.... The conversation went roughly like this (in Sorkin's words):

Me: I'm pretty excited about this.

Manager: Well, no one does this type of thing like Sorkin.

Me: This is my return to television—it's the only way to go.

Manager: The offer is the only issue.

Me: What is the offer? What exactly is it?

Manager: The offer is for one episode....

Me: I'm aware of it. Thank you very much. What's the number, I meant?

Manager's fee is $50,000 every episode.

Me: I got over a million dollars for Friends. Can't we persuade them to stand? Manager: It doesn't appear to be so. They want this to be a true ensemble show, so they're giving it to everyone.

Me: I can't believe I'm having to decline the best television screenplay I've ever read. God thank my management for not giving up. He informed the producers that, while Studio 60 on the Sunset Strip was intended to be an ensemble production, as soon as I came onstage, it would be all about my character, which is exactly what happened. We got them off their ensemble idea after roughly six weeks of negotiating with that argument in mind. We negotiated a fee of $175,000 for me to be billed as the show's star. That is certainly an incredible amount of money to be paid per week, but three steps down, LeBlanc was being paid $600,000 per week to play Joey. However, the writing won out (every actor is only searching for excellent material), and I accepted the lowball offer (and they hired my good friend Amanda Peet to complete out the cast).

We shot the pilot, and I'd put him up against any pilot I'd ever seen—he was that excellent. There was an intensity to it, a crackle that is uncommon in television, and fans enjoyed it as well. It had a massive opening. (All of my shows after Friends were huge at first, but then they weren't.) The second episode of Studio 60 received around half as many viewers as the first. Nobody was interested in the show. It took me a long time to figure out why. Studio 60 on the Sunset Strip had a fatal weakness that no amount of superb writing, direction, or performance could overcome. The stakes were as high as you could imagine on The West Wing: a nuclear weapon is aiming at Ohio, and the president has to solve that shit? People in Ohio would watch such a show merely to see what would happen if they were encouraged to kiss their own asses goodbye by an impending intercontinental ballistic missile.

A very limited group of people, including myself, understand that getting a joke right is a matter of life and death in a certain industry. These are warped, strange folks. People in Canton, Ohio, watching Studio 60 on the Sunset Strip, on the other hand, presumably thought, It's just a joke, why isn't everyone calm down? What's the big deal, what's the problem with all of you? This was not the Monty Python sketch about Ernest Scribbler writing a joke so amusing that it murdered Nazis. (Because they don't know German, the British are immune to its force. And the killer joke's actual German is nonsense, which is equally amusing.) There may have been a loyal audience in Rock Center or at the Comedy Store on Sunset, but the main premise of the act didn't reach the levels of edge-of-your-seat stakes. Trying to tie the stakes of The West Wing to a comedic program would never succeed.

On a more specific level, I found the work environment at Studio 60 on the Sunset Strip to be frustratingly different from that of Friends or even The Whole Nine Yards. Aaron runs a tight ship—just the way he likes it—to the point where there was someone on site with a script making sure that if the original reads "he is angry" and I, or someone else, condensed it to "he's angry," we'd have to reshoot the entire scene—it had to be done exactly as written. (I dubbed the production assistant whose job this was "the Hawk," and what an awful job she had, having to be a hall monitor to a bunch of creative individuals who were playing their balls off.) Unfortunately, even if a take with a little different rendering of the line was the best of all, the one that was utilised was the word-perfect one, not the best. The Aaron Sorkin / Tommy Schlamme system was never really actor based, so it was much more about getting the text correct, as if it were Shakespeare—in fact, I overheard someone on set suggest that this was Shakespeare....

I also had a different perspective on the creative process in general—I was used to offering ideas, but Aaron rejected all of them. I had opinions about my character's arc as well, but they were not welcomed. The issue is that I'm not just a talking head. I have a brain, especially when it comes to comedy. Aaron Sorkin is a far better writer than I am, but he is not a funnier man (he once claimed that Friends was his favourite show). In Studio 60, I played a comedy writer. I thought I had some amusing ideas, but Aaron said no to all of them. That's his prerogative, and it's no reflection on him that he prefers to do his set in this manner. It simply disappointed me. (Aaron did the same thing to Tom Hanks, according to him.) I suppose I was fortunate in that I'd already discovered that being on a popular TV show didn't make things better. The show took off like a rocket, with the pilot drawing a whopping thirteen million viewers and a fourteen share. The reviews were also positive. "It's difficult not to root for Studio 60 on the Sunset Strip," stated Variety, "a series that marries Aaron Sorkin's crackling dialogue and willingness to tackle big ideas with a beyond-stellar cast." The Chicago Tribune went even farther, writing me a love letter in which they stated, "Studio 60 is not just good, it has the potential to be a small-screen classic."

However, the issue remained: it was attempting to be a serious show about comedy and superb television, as if those two things were as significant as world politics. On the Onion's A.V. Club vertical, I recently read an extremely insightful assessment of Studio 60. Its author, Nathan Rabin, agrees that the pilot was a great piece of work, writing a few years after the show debuted. I, like most of the general public, awaited the premiere of the pilot with bated breath on September 18, 2006. I couldn't wait to see what occurred next once it was over. I watched it again... a few months ago [and] what struck me the most on a second viewing was its endless feeling of possibilities. Studio 60 has the potential to go anywhere. It has the potential to do anything. And it might be able to accomplish so with one of the most impressive casts in recent memory. The pilot for Studio 60 still has potential, even if it was doomed to go terminally unmet the second time around.

But, as Rabin points out, the show arguably took itself too seriously, given that it was intended to be about jokes, and Sorkin's complete control of the program left no place for anybody else to breathe. The vanity of the show extended to having Aaron Sorkin write every episode. Staff writers were given "story by" credits here and there, but Studio 60 was essentially a one-man show. Sorkin's voice takes centre stage.... [I]n its own peculiar way, Studio 60 survives, albeit as an immense, occasionally interesting folly rather than a grand masterpiece. Times had changed as well. We debuted just as television was evolving into a new species. "Appointment TV," like Friends or The West Wing, was on its way out. People were recording broadcasts to watch later, which damaged ratings, which became the show's story rather than the show itself, which was otherwise excellent. By the end of the first — and only —season, viewers had largely agreed with Rabin's judgement, and we were down to four million watchers, with only 5% of TVs turned in. We were lost. I wasn't heartbroken by my lack of success since, as I previously indicated, I knew a hit TV program couldn't complete my soul. In any event, something else was occupying my mind.

"Friends with benefits" had turned into love after two years. This was one of the "normal" times in my life. True, every now and then I'd stumble and take two OxyContin, after which I'd have to detox for six days. But the relationship had progressed to the point where I needed to ask her a question right away.

"I think we should stop kidding ourselves," I stated one day. "We love each other," she said, and she wasn't wrong. I was madly in love with her. However, our intimacy concerns were being overshadowed by the fact that we were both extremely dedicated to our jobs. My dread of her leaving was still there, and who knows, maybe she was afraid of me leaving her.

Nonetheless, the moment arrived. I'd paid a lot of money for an artist to paint the two of us for Christmas. Our relationship had always been sex- and text-driven—at least for the first four years—and I'd learned from my company manager that we'd exchanged around 1,780 texts. So, in the painting, she was sitting down with a copy of The New York Times and some bottled water, as she always did, and I was on the bottom left, wearing a long sleeve T-shirt with another T-shirt on top of it, as I always did, holding a Red Bull and reading a Sports Illustrated... and we were texting each other the whole time. The artist had added 1,780 hearts, one for each phrase, then smashed them all together to form a single large heart. I'd never spent so much money on a present before. I adored her and wanted her to know it. My objective was to present her with the painting before asking her the question. You know the one; I'm not going to tell you how it goes, especially because... well, I never asked. When I gave her the gift, she was moved, saying, "Matty, my little heart—what you're doing to my little heart."

And the time had come. "Honey, I love you," was all I had to say. Will you..." But I didn't say anything. All my concerns reared up like a serpent, the snake I dreaded would come after me the year before I met her, the period when I'd seen God but didn't learn enough from him. I got into Chandler fucking Bing mode right away.

"Hey, hey, hey!" says someone. "Look at this!" I exclaimed, bringing back that stupid Chandler cadence one last time.

I had missed the opportunity. Who knows, maybe she was anticipating it. I'd been seconds; seconds and a lifetime away. If I'd asked, now we'd have two kids and a house with no view, who knows—I wouldn't need the view since I'd have her to look at, as well as the kids. Instead, I'm some schmuck sitting alone in his house at fifty-three, staring down at a hushed sea.... So I didn't inquire. I was either too terrified, too shattered, or too bent. I'd been completely faithful to her for the entire time, including the last two years, during which I didn't want to have sex with her for some reason, during which no amount of couples therapy could explain why I'd never asked the damn question, and why I now only saw her as my best friend. My pal; my dearest pal. And I didn't want to lose my best friend, so I tried for two years to make it work. I had no idea why the sex had ceased. I have this creeping, nagging, never-ending concern that if we grew any closer, she'd see the true me and leave me. I didn't like myself at the time, you see. Our age gap had also become an issue. She was always wanting to get out and do things, but I desired a more established life.

But there were other concerns. Her focus on her profession collided with my approach to life at the moment, which was to do nothing. I was practically retired—I didn't think I'd ever work again. I was ridiculously wealthy, so I spent my time playing video games and hanging out with myself. But what was I supposed to do now?

Accept effort. Mr. Sunshine is a TV show I produced. I believe that life is about the journey, not the destination, and because I had not yet written, this was my first attempt. Writing a network show about something you want to write about is nearly impossible. There are so many cooks in the kitchen—executives and other writers who all want a say—that the reality of your true vision getting to the screen is reserved only for someone like Sorkin. Mr. Sunshine revolves around my character, Ben Donovan, who owns and operates a sports facility in San Diego; Allison Janney plays my supervisor. One of Ben's major flaws is his unwillingness to make himself attractive to women.... After the titles, I even managed to get in an inside joke: my production firm was called "Anhedonia Productions," and the ad card we designed included a cartoon of me moaning with boredom on a roller coaster. Despite my efforts, the show was a tremendous hit for about two weeks before everyone in the world decided they didn't want to watch it. But it had been a very beneficial experience since I had learned how to create a television show from the ground up. It's one of those things that appears simple but is actually quite difficult, similar to algebra or having a real discussion with another human being. I had a good time, but it was a marathon and I'm a sprinter. And it soon transformed a sober, video game-playing rich man into an extremely busy man, which was not a good thing. In reality, the show swiftly took precedence over my sobriety, and as a result, I relapsed once more.

I'd Go On to make another program (oh, yeah, that's what it was called, Go On) about a sports talk radio broadcaster dealing with the loss of his wife. NBC kept promoting it, even airing it during the Olympics, and sixteen million people saw the premiere. But a comedy about bereavement counselling? The finale drew only 2.5 million viewers in April 2013. Once again, a production I was directing had a fantastic opening but was cancelled. I relapsed once more because I had nothing to do and no one to love. But I noticed this one soon and checked into a recovery facility in Utah. It was there that I met Burton, a Yoda-like psychotherapist who informed me that I preferred the drama and mayhem of my drug problem. "What exactly are you talking about?" I inquired. "It's destroyed my life." It robbed me of everything nice I've ever had." I was quite irritated.

But what if he's correct?

CHAPTER 7

Odyssey

After Friends, after the movies, after that six-year relationship, after the collapse and rise and rise and fall—after everything—I found myself on an odyssey for the next six years. Contrary to popular belief, I was not a wealthy guy with nothing to do; in fact, I had more to do than before. No, I was a man tumbling down a slope, stranded in a roaring river, attempting to find refuge on any safe and dry rock.

I'd gone to Cirque Lodge in Sun Valley, Utah, between Mr. Sunshine and Go On—rehab number three, if you're keeping score at home. The Lodge is located in the Utah Rockies, near the base of Mount Timpanogos. I'm not a great fan of nature—in terms of peace and quiet, I prefer the beach, or at least a glimpse of the water—but this spot was breathtaking. The air was pure and thin, razor-sharp and clarifying. There were turkeys everywhere, gobbling to the bone (and flying once in a while—who knew they could fly?), golden eagles, and on some days, a moose would pass by, heavy and slow (no, I wasn't hallucinating; there were moose there).

Cirque Lodge was not only beautiful, but it also had a great staff who knew what they were doing. My counsellor Burton (who I would have thought was Yoda if his face was green) ended up being quite helpful to me—with both the genuine problems I brought with me and the manufactured ones I kept with me at all times. (He also happens to be one of the males I've ever said "I love you" to.) I arrived quite afraid (a requirement for entering rehab, but deeply unpleasant nonetheless), and Burton's calming voice immediately helped me feel a little better.

"Discover, uncover, and discard" was one of Cirque's primary mantras, and I was delighted to believe I could at least execute that last one—it was time to finally get rid of all this stuff. At this point, I was such an expert on the 12 steps (and everything else they tend to emphasise in treatment) that I spent a lot of my time at Cirque helping out the novices and trying to have a little fun. I had a Ping-Pong table brought in and even developed a game centred on a red ball that we hurled back and forth, which kept my fellow inmates entertained for hours and gave me a sense of purpose. I wanted to assist so much, and I was brilliant at it.

I was under the assumption that during my stay, I would have to undertake profound trauma therapy, going back into my childhood and retrieving all of my old anguish and loneliness, thereby starting the hard process of letting these things go. The notion was that if I got over these horrific situations, I wouldn't need drugs and alcohol to mask them.

Burton, on the other hand, had a different perspective. He accused me of enjoying the drama of my addiction and wondered how I could have so much fun at Cirque Lodge while being so upset by practically everything that happened in the real world.

This question irritated me right away. This appeals to me? How could Burton claim I appreciated my decades of addiction and terror, my lack of control, and my apparent inner torture? It was customary for participants to invite friends to come and visit during Family and Friends Week, but I resisted. My father had visited me at Hazelden, my mother at Promises Malibu, and my then-girlfriend had spent many hours watching me rant with a slew of house nurses and sober companions while detoxing. I didn't want to subject them to this again. It was too terrible, too difficult, and too unfair. It was the least I could do to give them a rest. I'd put myself into this mess, and I'd get myself out of it.

But one day, around Friends and Family Week, I found myself sitting outside by myself, hoping to see a moose or a bird flapping up into the trees. The day was bitterly cold, subzero, but I needed to smoke, so there was nothing for it except to bundle up and deal.... A light snow began to fall while I sat there puffing on a Marlboro, creating an intense quiet, as if the cosmos was patiently listening to my thoughts and emotions. I'm curious what the universe heard. I was thinking about why I hadn't wanted any visitors during this stay when something important occurred to me.... Why am I allowing my family and loved ones to go through this torment but not myself?

With that realisation, I knew Burton's counsel was correct—I did enjoy the turmoil. It was time to take a breather. Drugs hadn't given me what I wanted in a long time, but I kept returning to them, putting my life in danger in order to... what? Escape? What are you trying to get away from? The worst thing I had to flee was my alcoholism and addiction, thus using alcohol and drugs to do so... Well, you can see the logical impossibility. Nothing made sense, not even the slightest. I was smart enough to see it; doing something about it, on the other hand... that was a new level of maths for me. Even when your life is at stake, change can be frightening.

But, at the very least, I was finally asking smart questions, even if the answers weren't always obvious. Deep down, I realised that life is about the simple pleasures like throwing a red ball back and forth and watching a moose lope across a clearing. I needed to let myself off the hook for everything that was causing the damage, such as still being furious with my parents, being unattended all those years ago, feeling inadequate, and being scared of commitment because I was terrified of the end of commitment.

I needed to remember that my father left because he was terrified, and my mother was just a youngster doing her best. It wasn't her fault she'd had to devote so much time to the fucking Canadian prime minister—even with a child at home, it was never going to be a nine-to-five job. But I couldn't see it back then, and now we're here....

I needed to move forward and upward, to comprehend that there was a large world out there that wasn't out to get me. In reality, it didn't have an opinion about me. The universe was impartial, beautiful, and continued with or without me, just like the animals and the shiv-sharp air. In fact, I was living in a society where, despite its neutrality, I had managed to carve out an important, meaningful place for myself. I needed to know that when I died, I didn't want my Friends to be near the bottom of my list of accomplishments. I needed to remind myself to be courteous to people, to make their bumping into me a pleasant experience rather than one that filled me with dread, as if that was all that counted. I needed to be more kind, to love more deeply, to listen more carefully, and to give unreservedly. It was time to quit being such a fearful asshole and accept that I would be able to manage whatever problems arose. Because I was powerful.

The snow eventually stopped falling, and a moose crept gently into the gardens. That lengthy face seemed placid, as if it had seen everything at least once and wasn't fazed by anything. That had a lesson in it, I reasoned. A few calves kept up with her, full of the vitality that only children have. They all gazed at me as they sat in the twilight, then turned and walked away.

Perhaps this was the message from the universe. I didn't matter in the grand scheme of things. I was just another human being spinning in circles.

That was enough for me to learn. I stubbed out the Marlboro and returned to the game room to lead yet another round of Red Ball.

I left Cirque Lodge lean and joyful, eager to take on the world and spend the rest of my life with my love. But my then-girlfriend didn't like this new Matty—I got the impression she didn't enjoy the fact that I needed her less than before. Perhaps my issues had given her a false sense of security. This guy will never leave me, not while he is so preoccupied with his own issues. She didn't like the fact that I was better. That unpleasant truth proved to be our undoing. We gave up after trying so hard to fit the individual pieces together. Everything was depressing. She was my absolute favourite person in the world, but it was not to be. It was the proper thing to do, but it wasn't without sadness.

What now, yet again?

I originally filled the void with activism, but in doing so, I flew too close to the sun and managed to lose my last shred of innocence.

I'd spent time at Promises, a rehab in Malibu, in 2001 (just after picking up AA's Big Book in Marina del Rey). I met a guy named Earl H. there. He'd been teaching a class at Promises, and I'd loved him right away. He was amusing and quite informed about AA. He also had a few other celebrity clients who were doing well, so I figured he'd be my guy and asked him to sponsor me. (He claimed he hadn't drank since 1980.) Over coffee, I confessed that one of my fears was that he'd pass me a script to read one day. "Well, there is a script, but I wouldn't do that to you," he added.

So our connection began. I practised the steps with him, even chasing him down to complete them. I was so desperate to get into the program and stay sober that I called him every day and asked for a job. Nobody had ever followed him harder, he claimed, and over the next ten years, he came to wear two hats—he was my sponsor, but he was also my best friend. I turned to face him and listened to him. We had the same sense of humour and even sounded similar. I ignored the idea that he was somewhat famous in the rehab world, a world where everything should be kept private.

But my biggest blunder was that I had made him my higher authority. If I had a problem with a relationship or anything else, I would call him, and he would be extremely wise about it. It got to the point where if he'd said, "I'm sorry, Matthew, but you have to move to Alaska and stand on your head," I'd have booked a ticket to Anchorage right now. If he'd said, "You can eat nothing but green

M&M's for the next three months," you could bet I'd be shitting khaki.

I knew deep down that making your sponsor your best buddy was a poor idea, but Earl was everything to me. He'd become my father, my mentor. I'd go see him speak (he was a hilarious and extremely effective public speaker), and we'd go to the movies together. When I relapsed, he would assist me with finding treatment centres. It's hardly an exaggeration to say he saved my life multiple times.

Then our friendship evolved into a business. Yes, I started a business with my sponsor. Fucking fatal error.

Earl had founded a corporation that would build and operate sober living homes throughout Los Angeles. I put $500,000 into the firm and converted my Malibu home into Perry House, a sober living facility. Earl and I travelled to Washington, DC multiple times to speak with lawmakers to promote the efficacy of drug courts, at the request of a terrific person named West Huddleston, the head of the National Association of Drug Court Professionals. Drug courts seek to decriminalise nonviolent addicts by providing them with care and therapy rather than jail time. Gil Kerlikowske, then Obama's "drug czar," even managed to award me a "Champion of Recovery award" from the Obama administration's Office of National Drug Control Policy in May 2013. At the time, I quipped to The Hollywood Reporter that "had I been arrested, I would be sitting in prison somewhere with a tattoo on my face."

That same month, I guest hosted Piers Morgan Live, speaking with Lisa Kudrow and Lauren Graham while also discussing addiction and recovery issues. I was trying to figure out what I wanted to do next, and I felt at ease doing the show. I started by claiming I wasn't Piers Morgan, and the only way to tell was that "I don't have a British accent, and I don't have a first name that sounds very pointy," which made Lisa laugh out loud. Maybe this is my future, I reasoned.

I even got to make a joke about my upcoming autobiography being titled Still a Boy.

Oops.

In any case, I was suddenly a talk show host as well as an award-winning addict. What the fuck happened there?

Earl had been scheduled to come on Piers Morgan with me but had backed out at the last minute. Nonetheless, we later travelled to Europe to increase the power of drug courts, and I had the opportunity to debate the matter on a late-night BBC news show called Newsnight. There was the moderator, Jeremy Paxman, who was known for being unpleasant to guests; Baroness Meacher, who was the then-chair of the UK All-Party Parliamentary Group on Drug Policy Reform and was very much on my side; and then a complete tool named Peter Hitchens.

I can't imagine what it's like to have a sibling who everyone adores when you're the foolish brother everyone despises, but Peter might be able to tell you. The loss of Peter's magnificent brother, the great Christopher Hitchens, reverberates still—an unrivalled raconteur, writer, arguer, and bon vivant—and the world mourns Christopher even now, more than a decade after his cruel death from cancer. Unfortunately, his younger brother, Peter, is still pontificating on topics he has no knowledge of, combining right-wing ideology with paternalism and moral tutting. Hitchens appeared on Newsnight to expound on his bizarre beliefs that drug use is simply a case of poor morals ("There's an enormous fashion at the moment," he sneered, "for dismissing the ability of people to take control of their own lives, and to make excuses for them," sounding like some insane great-aunt who'd had one too many glasses of sherry). Even stranger, he later "argued" that addiction does not exist. I'd like to think the baroness and I ran rings around him, but it wasn't difficult. Aside from pointing out that I expected him to show up to the interview wearing big-boy pants, but he clearly didn't, I also managed to repeatedly point out that the American Medical Association had diagnosed addiction as a disease in 1976, and that he was about the only person on the planet who disagreed with that assessment. He didn't like it, and the conversation eventually concluded with Paxman and Baroness Meacher laughing out loud at how dumb and harsh Hitchens sounded:

Hitchens: So, if what you claim is true, how do people ever stop being addicts?

Me: Okay, Santa...

Hitchens: That's extremely clever, but this is a very serious matter. And you do so with great levity… I assume he was proving that he knew nothing about me or the issue on which he was pontificating.

Meanwhile, despite making Peter Hitchens look like a fool and advocating for drug courts all over Europe, Perry House was floundering in the United States. Because there were not enough attendees—it was simply too expensive—I had to cut my losses and sell the property. I asked Earl for my money back at lunch, and I'm still waiting. He was fantasising of being an actress, among other things. Something was wrong, and I was so spooked out by it all that I went home and used it. This was entirely my fault, but two things were irreversibly lost: my innocence and my faith in Earl H.

Earl eventually moved to Arizona without telling me, and our friendship ended. I'd lost half a million dollars, my closest ally, and the innocence I'd cherished all those years by sharing our lives and being best friends and pushing for drug courts and constructing a sober living home. Heartbreak.

For years, I had been writing television with a collaborator. I was feeling extremely uneasy and ill at ease the day following the Earl H.

fiasco, and I remembered that a wise guy once advised me that at times like these, I should be creative. So I opened my laptop and began typing. I had no idea what I was typing. I simply continued typing. It became clear that what was being shown was a drama.

I needed this; I'd just let my standards slip severely, and I was determined to claw my way back to the point where I could consider looking in the mirror.

I was furious with myself for what had transpired on CBS's The Odd Couple. I'd been a tremendous fan of the film adaptation of Neil Simon's play for a long time and had always wanted to develop a new TV version of it. My goal came true in 2013, when CBS approved the concept. Go On, my previous show before The Odd Couple, had failed, but I was more certain about this one. The original material was amazing, the cast was fantastic, and everything was in place for a hit. Nonetheless, despair followed me, and my addictions returned in full force. As a result, I'm deeply humiliated by my actions on The Odd Couple. On top of the severe sadness, I was always late and high, and I eventually lost control of the program to a showrunner. But I accept full responsibility for what transpired and would like to apologise to everyone involved, not just my fellow castmates.

I had a play in mind with that calamity in the rearview mirror. When I felt that dis-ease, that discomfort flowing out of my flesh, I used medicines to replace it, to make myself feel better. But now that I was sober, I knew I couldn't do it—I needed to find something else. I wrote ten hours a day for ten days straight until I finished the play—which, according to the few people I allowed to see it, was actually rather good. I'd titled it The End of Longing, and despite the fact that it took me ten days to write, I spent another year refining it.

I'd been inspired by—and by inspired, I mean I was aiming to beat—Sexual Perversity in Chicago, and I was pleased with my results. I'd take it over that wonderful play any day. "There's a very popular notion that people don't change," I'd told The Hollywood Reporter, "but I see people change every day, and I wanted to put that message out there while making people laugh." As a result, the play opens with four buddies in a bar seeking to find love—my character, Jack, begins the play as an egomaniac who also happens to be an alcoholic, and things only go worse from there.

I was not satisfied with simply writing a play; I felt it needed to be presented and starred myself. The End of Longing opened months later in London's prestigious West End theatre area. I liked being both the playwright and the lead because I could change things up when they weren't working. And, while I knew I'd detest doing the huge drunk scene every night—it was bound to be incredibly triggering—I also knew I had to demonstrate just how low a person can go.

We debuted in the Playhouse Theatre, a facility with a capacity of 800 people, and promptly sold out. In fact, we were breaking box office records while also receiving poor reviews. There were seven important reviews for historical accuracy, six of which were negative. The thought of a Hollywood actor-boy performing a play in London did not sit well with London critics. But it was a big hit, and I was a playwright who liked the notion.

There was also one person who refused to attend the play, despite my entreaties.

The woman I'd dated for six years was now dating a British guy, and they were splitting their time between London and Los Angeles. We'd had a few meals and texted a few times while we were still friendly. I'd offered to see The End of Longing when she was in London, but she'd texted back saying she was far too busy. "I'll see you Stateside!" she wrote. I answered that I was disappointed that she couldn't make it—the play was being played in her town, for God's sake—and then I received an email saying that she was getting married and that she had no room in her life for friends. I didn't respond to that email, and we haven't communicated since. It was a brutal way to break the news that she was getting married, and it's not something I'd ever do to a person, but there you have it. Even so, I'll be in her corner for the rest of my life. I'm delighted she got married and is content. I want nothing but the best for her in the future.

The play was relocated from London to New York. That was not a good time. For starters, I had to tone down the play—the Brits didn't mind the salty language, but Broadway is Broadway, so I had to leave it, and not just the language—I had to kill a lot of the comedy as well. So it wasn't well received or beloved in New York—the New York Times destroyed it, calling it "synthetic," whatever that means, and I only made $600 for the entire New York run. That is not a typo. (I'd made a thousand times more—nearly to a pound, shilling, and pence—during its run in London.) At the very least, The Hollywood Reporter was complimentary: "Perry at least demonstrates that his extensive television comedy experience has rubbed off." The evening is filled with funny one-liners (the most of which are, inevitably, delivered by the author)..... Perry exhibits his trademark great comic timing and delivery." But the "at least" was crushing, and I understood that The End of Longing wasn't going to be popular enough to secure my future as a developing David Mamet. But there is still time!

CHAPTER 8

Three's Not Company, Three Ruins Everything

When a man or woman asks me to help them quit drinking, and I do it, seeing as the light slowly returns to their eyes, that's all God to me. And, even though I have a relationship with God and am often grateful despite everything, I sometimes want to tell God to go fuck himself for making my path so difficult.

When I'm clean and sober, it's as if a light has been turned on for me, one that I can share with a desperate man who needs help quitting drinking. It's the same light that glistens on the ocean in bright sunlight. That is what God is to me. (It also works at night when the moonlight hits the water—boom! It almost knocks me over. Because, like that five-year-old youngster travelling across a continent alone, seeing the city lights of Los Angeles and knowing he is about to be parented... well, it's all the same.)

Why is it so difficult for me to stay sober when I see my peers doing it so easily? Why has my path been so difficult? Why have I struggled so much with life? Why has truth been an acquired taste, and why has it been so difficult for me to acquire? But when I help that one man become sober, or even thousands of people get sober on a weekend at a retreat or conference, all of these questions fade away. It's as though I'm standing under a Hawaiian waterfall, getting bathed by the delicious warm water. That's where God is; you'll simply have to trust me on that.

I'm no saint—none of us are—but if you've gone to the brink of death and don't die, you'd think you'd be filled with relief and thanks. But that isn't the case; instead, you are frustrated by the difficult road ahead of you to become healthier. Something else happens as well. You're haunted by the question, "Why have I been spared?" The other four patients on the ECMO machine were still dead. There had to be a reason.

My ten thousand hours in AA and helping people become sober was part of the answer for me. That brightens me up, lends me a little of the golden light from my kitchen.

But there has to be more, God. Why did you save me? I'm ready to go—just point me in the right path. When Woody Allen poses this inquiry to an alien in the film Stardust Memories, the creature says, "Tell funnier jokes." But that can't be right.

In any case, I'm ready. And I look for the answer every day. I am a seeker. I am looking for God.

My romantic life, on the other hand, is a very different tale. I've made more blunders in my love life than Elizabeth Taylor. I am a romantic and passionate person. I feel a need for love that I cannot fully articulate.

The regulations had changed by the time I reached my forties. I'd done all the sleeping with individuals I'd ever need to do—now I was seeking for a partner, a comrade, someone to share my life with. I've also always had a soft spot for children. I guess it's because my sister Caitlin was born when I was eleven years old. Then came Emily, Will, and eventually Madeline. I enjoyed playing with them all, babysitting them and playing silly games with them. There is no more beautiful sound on the globe than a child's laughter.

So, by the time my forties kicked in, I was desperate for a partner, someone I could rely on and who, in turn, could rely on me. One night, a group of friends and I went out to celebrate yet another year of sobriety. My old friend David Pressman introduced me to his girlfriend's sister, Laura. We'd all gone to a Dodgers game together, but there was no game, no stadium, no hot dog vendors for me—the world had receded to a lovely face behind a baseball cap. I attempted to use my old Perry charm—anything to get her attention—but she was too busy flaunting her amazing personality and wit to others. She was underwhelmed that I was Chandler, and though she was absolutely cordial to me, I had the impression there was no there-there for her. I delivered a speech to myself as I drove home that night.

"Yes, you're disappointed, but not every girl is going to like you, Matty." I let things go, but I didn't forget about her. Surely, our paths would meet again.

And they did. This time, the party opted to play Ping-Pong at the Standard Hotel in downtown Los Angeles. Now, I'm no Forrest Gump, but I know my way around a Ping-Pong table—in fact, if you've seen the season nine finale of Friends, you'll know that I'm good enough to beat Paul Rudd. I knew Laura may show up, so I played Ping-Pong with one eye on the door.

Finally, she appeared. She was all energy and humour, as if she had been thrown into the club by a whirlwind.

"Everyone in here should kill themselves," Laura said, and BOOM! like a block of curiosity slammed into my face. But I was prepared this time. So began a night that resembled a knife fight, but with jokes instead of knives. My new love turned out to be a stand-up comedian and a renowned television writer. We knew right once that we'd never run out of things to say to each other.

Our first date took place on New Year's Eve. I asked Laura to a pyjama party that a buddy was throwing. After that, our relationship grew slowly; she was cautious, and I was eager to go to any length. But our feelings grew stronger. It was all good... but nothing is ever perfect in my world, remember?

Enter the city of Rome. I had been clean for two years and was prospering in AA, healthy, sponsoring people, and developing a TV show. I was ecstatic, even muscular, dare I say. (I dare: I'd been working out in the gym!) I was requested to speak at an AA meeting in West Hollywood, and you can't say no to an AA request. The place was full, with standing room only (I believe news had spread that I was speaking). My story had not yet reached the depths of the last few years, so in addition to recounting everything I'd gone through, I was able to get my fair share of chuckles. I went over to the kitchen area at one point and spotted a woman peering through the window/hatch contraption, leaning on her elbows to prop herself up. She was stunningly attractive and like a wonderful porcelain doll. There were suddenly only two people in the room. My AA contribution became solely aimed towards Rome. It turned out to be one of the best shares I'd ever given since this magnificent beauty captivated me so much that I wanted her to know everything about me. I wanted her to be aware of everything.

Following that, as we all met outside for a cigarette, we began talking and flirting.

"So, what are you up to right now?" she said.

"I'm going home to write." "I've suddenly become a writer," I explained.

"Well," Rome replied, "I'd make an excellent muse."

"I'll bet you do," I answered as I turned and walked away, thoroughly taken aback by this odd individual.

I gave myself a pep talk on the drive home. What about Laura, though? Yes, of course, gorgeous Laura, whom I am growing more fond of by the day. But now we have Rome. What is a guy to do?

Forget about Rome and keep looking into this Laura thing that is going so beautifully. Right? That's what a reasonable person would do in these circumstances.

However, Rome had cast a spell on me. Despite my good self-talk, this is when I made a fatal mistake. I didn't realise it was a mistake at the time—do any of us realise we're making mistakes while we're making them? Maybe we wouldn't make them if we didn't?

The problem, and it was a big one, was that I started dating both women. This is not a move I would suggest under any circumstances, but particularly if you are me. I told myself that I wasn't being an asshole because I hadn't told either Laura or Rome that we were in a relationship, but there was a part of me that knew I was doing something wrong because I cared about both of them, and despite outward appearances, I genuinely didn't want anyone to get hurt, including myself. So Laura and I would go to Kings games together, laugh, and have a fantastic, albeit somewhat chaste, time. The relationship with both ladies was sluggish at first, but they ultimately lifted their sex embargoes, and I was now totally involved with two distinct women at the same time. It was incredible, as well as perplexing and bizarre.

Did I mention I was madly in love with both of them? I didn't believe that was even feasible. I even went online and read a few stories to confirm that this had truly occurred. According to what I read, the sentiments I had for each of these ladies were genuine. Then Laura and I declared ourselves boyfriend and girlfriend, while Rome and I did not—but I was still in trouble.

What did I intend to do? I had a great time with both of them. They were fantastic. This carried on for almost six months before I realised I needed to choose one. I had to put an end to this madness and choose one. Rome was passionate, sexy, humorous, and intelligent, but she also seemed to have a preoccupation with death, which perplexed me. Laura talked about movies and lighter topics; she made me feel at ease in a way that Rome had not.

Laura was my choice.

I made the tough phone call to Rome. She was OK about it at first, until she wasn't, yelling at me for two hours in the parking lot of Barney's Beanery on Santa Monica Boulevard when I tried to make amends. You'd be hard pressed to find an angrier person than she was that day with me.

But you know me by now; you know I can't stand growing closer and closer to someone, and that's exactly what was happening with Laura. Fear was infiltrating my body. Breaking up with Laura would be insane—she had everything. We had everything. We were the best of friends. But the intimacy terrified me. I knew that if she got to know me any better, she'd realise what I already knew about myself: I wasn't enough. It didn't matter who I was. She would soon realise this for herself and leave me. That would completely destroy me, and I would never recover.

There was an alternative. I could stay in the relationship while returning to drugs and attempting to maintain a low habit. This would shield me from the fear, allowing me to let down my guard and get more personal with her.

For me, turning to narcotics has resulted in nothing but mayhem. And yet, inexplicably, I chose to do it again to deal with the Laura problem. I began taking one tablet every day just to stay in the relationship. It was amazing at first, but as is always the case with drugs, they inevitably win. We had a shitstorm on our hands six months later. I was in shambles. Laura broke up with me, so I had to restart Suboxone and enter into a sober living facility. I was terrified that I was going to die again. Rome was still ranting at me whenever she could, and Laura was wounded, worried, and gone.

Oh, the magazines claimed something else about being in love with two individuals at the same time. It always comes to the same conclusion.

You lose both of them.

So there I was, living in a sober living house in Malibu on 8 milligrams of Suboxone. Though it is a great detox drug—the best, in my opinion—it is the most difficult drug to go off of. In fact, coming off it made me suicidal. That's not entirely accurate—I had suicidal thoughts, but I also realized it was just the medicine, so I wasn't genuinely suicidal. All I had to do was wait out the days when I felt suicidal, do nothing about it, and trust that eventually I would feel better and no longer want to kill myself.

To get off Suboxone, you must reduce your dose by one milligram every week until you reach zero. This causes you to feel quite ill for two days, after which you adjust to the new level—in this case, 7 milligrams—and then drop again. Suicidal thoughts do not appear until you are down to 2 mg.

So, at 2 milligrams, I probably performed the most selfish act in my life. I was frightened of how I was going to feel, and I didn't want to experience it alone. As a result, I bought $300 worth of flowers, drove to Laura's house, and begged her to take me back. We sat on the couch in her living room and spoke about what this would entail. I told her I wanted to marry her and perhaps have a kid with her, despite my dread.

Then something unbelievable happened. I heard a key gently turning in the front door as we sat there... and Rome entered.

Who walked in now?

How could these two women have been in the same room at the same time? I'd give anything to be able to travel back in time and say, "How about a threesome?" But now was not the time for jokes. My jaw had dropped to the floor.

"I'm going to water the plants," Rome remarked, and she disappeared up the rear stairway.

Laura remarked, "I think I need to take care of her," and left me in the living room. When I knew she wasn't coming back, I returned to Malibu with my 2-milligram addiction.

Rome and Laura had met at an AA meeting, discovered who they were, and quickly became good friends. As you can expect, the majority of their conversations revolved around what a jerk I was.

I couldn't stay in Los Angeles any longer, so I boarded a private plane to a Colorado recovery center where they stated they hoped they could wean me off Suboxone without making me suicidal.

So much for that notion. I felt suicidal for 36 days in a row before flying to New York and appearing on Letterman, trying to hide the fact that I was being held up with tape and paper.

I managed to pull it off.

Seven years later, after learning a lot about myself, I made genuine reparations to both Rome and Laura, and they both accepted my apology. Believe it or not, the three of us have become friends. Laura is married to a wonderful man named Jordan, and Rome is married to an equally wonderful man named Eric.

We just had supper together at my house, and we all had a great time. The two couples then drove away in their respective cars at approximately 10:00 p.m. I could hear the engines fading down the canyon toward the city.

Out back, as I waited for something to come to me, anything that may make things better, I heard the sound of coyotes once more.

No, it's just me, alone, fighting the monsters for one more night. They'd triumphed. And I knew I'd lost when I returned to my lonely bedroom to fight those demons and negotiate sleep once more.

CHAPTER 9

The Big Terrible Thing

Consider this: you have to walk back onto a stage where you have literally spit the bed for weeks. You've been slurring lines and making terrible decisions. You're in New York City, and despite having not one but two sober companions, you contact room service at the hotel, your voice shaking, detoxing, and say, "Please put a bottle of vodka in my room's bathtub." The bathtub, to be precise. Put that in there."

And then, when the day is done, you go back to that fucking hotel room, drink the bottle of vodka, and you feel okay for about three hours before having to do it all over again the next day. You're trembling and pretending that you're not in serious trouble anytime you speak to anyone. You contact the hotel and instruct them to perform the vodka-bottle-in-the-bathtub thing again, using the same nervous voice.

This is something that a "normy"—what we addicts call all you lucky nonalcoholics—might never fully grasp. I'll try to explain: if you drink an entire bottle of vodka, you get really sick the next day. A couple beers in the morning helped, but because I was the star in a major studio film, I couldn't drink in the morning. You're ill and trembling, and it feels like every part of your body is fighting to escape. And that's for the entire day—the entire fourteen-hour day.

The only way to get better is to drink the same amount, or a bit more, the next night. "So just don't drink," the normy advises. We alcoholics believe that if we don't drink, we would go insane—not to mention that the alcoholic will be even sicker, and appear even sicker, if he doesn't drink the bottle.

"But what about the movie?" says one.

It doesn't matter because I have to drink.

"How about taking a break for the night?"

It is not possible.

What's the next question?

So here I am in Dallas, on methadone, a quart of vodka every day, cocaine, and Xanax. Every day, I'd arrive on set, pass out in my chair, wake up to do a scene, stumble to set, and then scream into a camera for two minutes. Then it was back to my recliner for more snoozing.

I was one of the most renowned individuals in the world at the time, and I was being scorched by the white-hot flame of fame. As a result, no one dared to speak up about this heinous behaviour. The film's producers planned to finish the picture, slap my name on a banner, and make $60 million. Friends were even worse—no one wanted to interfere with that money-making machine.

During the production of Serving Sara, I considered taking Valium to help me relax. A doctor came to my duplex hotel room to provide medicines. I had drunk a party-size bottle of vodka with a handle the night before he came to visit. When the doctor looked around the room, he noticed the bottle and nervously said, "Did you drink all of that?"

"Yes," I responded, "may I have the Valium every four hours, not every six?"

He then turned tail and dashed down the spiral staircase and out the door, presumably to avoid being in the room if Matthew Perry died.

But, after Jamie Tarses informed me that I was leaving, I went to rehab and eventually returned to finish the film.

This was me as I was serving Sara. I was in shambles. I felt terrible, and I apologised to everyone, and I like to think I did a fantastic job for the final thirteen days of filming. Everyone tried to be nice about it, and they did their best, but they were irritated; the director was irritated—I'd damaged his movie; Elizabeth Hurley, my co-star, was irritated (she never got to do another movie, either).

I needed to make genuine amends, which is what AA teaches you. So I rerecorded my slurred parts for the entire film—which meant looping the entire film for days and days in a sound studio. In a studio, three beeps and I'd say my line to match my mouth. I'm really good at it, and we at least took the slurring out of the movie. Then I resolved to do as much press as possible in the history of press, bending over backwards to set things right. I was on the cover of every magazine and was on every talk show you can think of.

Consider this: you have to walk back onto a stage where you have literally spit the bed for weeks. You've been slurring lines and making terrible decisions. You're in New York City, and despite having not one but two sober companions, you contact room service at the hotel, your voice shaking, detoxing, and say, "Please put a bottle of vodka in my room's bathtub." The bathtub, to be precise. Put that in there."

And then, when the day is done, you go back to that fucking hotel room, drink the bottle of vodka, and you feel okay for about three hours before having to do it all over again the next day. You're trembling and pretending that you're not in serious trouble anytime you speak to anyone. You contact the hotel and instruct them to perform the vodka-bottle-in-the-bathtub thing again, using the same nervous voice.

This is something that a "normy"—what we addicts call all you lucky nonalcoholics—might never fully grasp. I'll try to explain: if you drink an entire bottle of vodka, you get really sick the next day. A couple beers in the morning helped, but because I was the star in a major studio film, I couldn't drink in the morning. You're ill and trembling, and it feels like every part of your body is fighting to escape. And that's for the entire day—the entire fourteen-hour day.

The only way to get better is to drink the same amount, or a bit more, the next night. "So just don't drink," the normy advises. We alcoholics believe that if we don't drink, we would go insane—not to mention that the alcoholic will be even sicker, and appear even sicker, if he doesn't drink the bottle.

"But what about the movie?" says one.

It doesn't matter because I have to drink.

"How about taking a break for the night?"

It is not possible.

What's the next question?

So here I am in Dallas, on methadone, a quart of vodka every day, cocaine, and Xanax. Every day, I'd arrive on set, pass out in my chair, wake up to do a scene, stumble to set, and then scream into a camera for two minutes. Then it was back to my recliner for more snoozing.

I was one of the most renowned individuals in the world at the time, and I was being scorched by the white-hot flame of fame. As a result, no one dared to speak up about this heinous behaviour. The film's producers planned to finish the picture, slap my name on a banner, and make $60 million. Friends were even worse—no one wanted to interfere with that money-making machine.

During the production of Serving Sara, I considered taking Valium to help me relax. A doctor came to my duplex hotel room to provide medicines. I had drunk a party-size bottle of vodka with a handle the night before he came to visit. When the doctor looked around the room, he noticed the bottle and nervously said, "Did you drink all of that?"

"Yes," I responded, "may I have the Valium every four hours, not every six?"

He then turned tail and dashed down the spiral staircase and out the door, presumably to avoid being in the room if Matthew Perry died.

But, after Jamie Tarses informed me that I was leaving, I went to rehab and eventually returned to finish the film.

This was me as I was serving Sara. I was in shambles. I felt terrible, and I apologised to everyone, and I like to think I did a fantastic job for the final thirteen days of filming. Everyone tried to be nice about it, and they did their best, but they were irritated; the director was irritated—I'd damaged his movie; Elizabeth Hurley, my co-star, was irritated (she never got to do another movie, either).

I needed to make genuine amends, which is what AA teaches you. So I rerecorded my slurred parts for the entire film—which meant looping the entire film for days and days in a sound studio. In a studio, three beeps and I'd say my line to match my mouth. I'm really good at it, and we at least took the slurring out of the movie. Then I resolved to do as much press as possible in the history of press, bending over backwards to set things right. I was on the cover of every magazine and was on every talk show you can think of.

The top page of The New York Times on July 19, 2019 carried items about Donald Trump, Stormy Daniels, a tragic arson at a Kyoto animation studio, and Puerto Ricans who had "had enough."

I had no idea about any of this. I wouldn't know anything for the next two weeks: El Chapo got life in prison plus thirty years; a nineteen-year-old shot three people dead (including himself) at a garlic festival in Gilroy, California; or Boris Johnson elected Prime Minister of the United Kingdom.

I was screaming when I awoke from my coma. My mum was present. I inquired as to what had occurred. She informed me that my colon had exploded.

"It's amazing that you're still alive," she exclaimed. "Your fortitude is admirable. And with some life modifications, you'll be OK. And the colostomy bag can be removed in around nine months."

I wondered if I had a colostomy bag. That's fantastic. That is a huge turn-on for girls.

I said, "Thank you very much."

After that, I rolled over and didn't speak or move for the next two weeks. I was on the verge of death due to what I had done. I was hooked up to fifty devices and would have to relearn how to walk.

I despised myself. I was on the verge of committing suicide. The embarrassment, loneliness, and sorrow were too much to bear. I just laid there, trying to deal with everything, but there was nothing I could do. It had already been completed. I was frightened of dying, which contradicted my activities.

But that was the end of it. The Matthew Perry Show has been cancelled due to opiates.

I could occasionally pay attention to what was going on in the room, but that was about it. I wasn't participating in anything. Chris and Brian Murray, two of my closest pals, would pay me a visit. Maria, my father's sister, came to see me about three weeks into it.

"Are you ready to hear about what happened?" she said.

I hardly nodded.

"After your colon exploded, they hooked you up to a ventilator, into which you vomited." So all of this bile and septic waste ended up in your lungs. They put you on an ECMO machine, and you lived. You were also in a coma for fourteen days."

I don't think I spoke for a week after that because I realised my worst nightmare had come true: I had done this to myself. But there was one bright spot. A fourteen-day coma makes quitting smoking incredibly easy.

I had been on and off opiates for so long that I had developed a condition that only a small percentage of the population experiences. Constipation is caused by opiates. It's almost poetry. I was so full of crap that I almost died.

In addition, I had a gastrointestinal problem.

"Don't leave me," I'd said to Erin just before the coma, as I was whirling on the ground in pain, immediately before I lost consciousness. I meant right then and there, but she took it literally, as did the rest of my friends and family. Erin worked the night shift in one hospital for five months. I often reflect on that time and am grateful that it occurred before Covid, because else I would have been trapped in that room for five months. As it turned out, I was never alone in that room. That was God's love manifested in human form.

My mother and I are both crisis experts at this point. What I've always wanted to tell her is that the show Friends, as well as all the other series and movies? I basically did anything for her attention. And yet, that is the one individual who did not receive much attention from Friends. She mentioned it on occasion, but she was never overjoyed with her son's accomplishments.

But I don't think she could possibly have been proud enough for what I required. And, if you're going to blame your parents for the terrible, you should equally give them credit for the good. Everything is good. I couldn't have played Chandler if my mother hadn't been my mother. I would never have made $80 million if it hadn't been for my mother. Because Chandler was only a mask for genuine pain. What a better sitcom character! Chandler began by making jokes about everything so we wouldn't have to talk about anything serious. Chandler was supposed to be "an observer of other people's lives" in the show's first description. So he'd be the man who, at the end of a play, would crack a joke or comment on whatever had just happened—the Fool in King Lear, uttering truth where none had previously existed. But everyone grew to like Chandler so much that he became his own significant character. That he ended up superseding what I did in real life—getting married, having kids—well, certain things I can't really talk about.

The simple truth is that when I was fifteen, I abandoned my mother, just as she had been abandoned by my father. I was a difficult child to deal with, and she, too, was a child. She constantly gave her all and stayed in my hospital room with me for five months following the coma.

When your colon explodes due to opiate overuse, the smart thing to do is not request pills to fix the problem... which is, of course, what I did.

And they handed them over to me.

I was hopelessly depressed and desperately wanted to feel better. Also, the hole in my stomach, large enough to fit a bowling ball, provided adequate reason to obtain pain medicine. Just so you know, I was on the verge of death due to opiates, and I begged the physicians to cure the situation with... opiates! So, no, even after the calamitous event, I was not finished. I hadn't discovered anything new. I still desired to use it.

I actually looked pretty decent when I got out of the hospital following the blast. I'd dropped a lot of weight, but I was so wounded that surgery to replace the bag couldn't be done for at least another nine months. So I returned to my flat and lied to everyone about the severity of my agony in order to obtain pain medication. I wasn't in any physical agony. It was more of a bother than a pain. Doctors, however, believed the deception and gave me a lot of opiates, and I obviously started smoking again.

And that was pretty much my existence.

Not to mention the colostomy bag was always breaking, leaving me with shit all over me at least fifty times.

Dear Colostomy Bag Manufacturers: Make a bag that doesn't break, you fucking moron. On Friends, did I make you laugh? If that's the case, please don't spit all over my face.

An addict feels elated after taking medication. However, after a short time, the pill no longer makes people feel euphoric because a tolerance has developed. But the addict still desperately wants to feel euphoric, so they take two instead of one to achieve the same effect.

When two is insufficient, they increase to three.

I used to play that little game till the number reached fifty-five pills per day. (Just watch the second half of Friends season three. I was fragile, emaciated, and unwell. It was obvious, but no one said anything about it.)

The UCLA hospital gave me opioids for my fabricated stomach discomfort, but I needed more, so I contacted a drug dealer. But I was on the forty-first level of that Century City building, which meant I had to find out a method to descend forty floors, give the dealer the money in an empty cigarette packet, and obtain my pills. Then I had to sneak back to the forty-first floor, take the medications, and feel better for a time.

Now I had to do it while living in the flat with a sober friend, a nurse, and Erin. It turned out I was lousy at it—I attempted four times and was caught each time. The UCLA physicians were not pleased and told me I needed to go to rehab.

I didn't have a choice because I was addicted to whatever they provided me. If I had just responded, "No, fuck off," it would have been a great moment, but the drugs would have stopped and I would have become quite ill. I was put in the unusual position of having to choose between being locked up in New York or Houston for months. Perhaps the decision should be made by someone more capable than me? I chose New York because I was the least qualified to make a selection.

When we arrived at the New York treatment centre, I was high as a kite and pretending to grip my stomach. Despite the fact that the environment resembled a prison, the people inside were cheerful.

"What the fuck are you guys so happy about?" I wondered. (I had a bad habit of being grouchy.) I was taking Ativan 14 milligrams and OxyContin 60 milligrams. I was using a colostomy bag. When I asked where I could smoke, I was told there was no smoking allowed.

"I won't be able to stay here if I can't smoke," I explained.

"Well, you obviously can't smoke here."

"I heard what you said." "How am I supposed to stop smoking on top of everything else?"

"We'll give you a patch."

"Don't blame me if I actually smoke the fucking patch," I added.

They agreed to keep me on Ativan, put me on Suboxone, and allow me to smoke throughout the detox but not while I was on the main unit. This meant I could smoke for another four days. When I wanted to smoke, a member of the staff would accompany me outside and stand next to me while I puffed away.

That was soothing.

After three nights, I met a very attractive and incredibly intelligent nurse. She took excellent care of me, and I flirted with her as much as you can with someone who changes your colostomy bag on a regular basis. The terrible day of having to quit smoking loomed, so I was allowed to go out for coffee with the great nurse. As a result, my mood improved slightly. We returned after I made jokes and flirted in the "we're all in rehab, so nothing can really happen" sort.

The nurse returned to the centre and said, "I need you to do something for me."

"Whatever you need," I told her.

"I need you to stop trying to fuck with the hot nurse."

She was talking about herself.

Jesus.

"I thought we were both flirting in a safe, never-going-to-happen kind of way," I explained.

I stayed for another four months and never flirted with her again. She also didn't flirt back at my non flirting, possibly because she'd seen me covered in my own excrement several times.

I stepped up to the ward and met therapists—Bruce, Wendy, whatever—who I despised. Everything I wanted to do was smoke. Or bring up the subject of smoking. Or smoke while discussing smoking.

Everyone resembled a massive cigarette.

I hardly ever left my room. The bag was constantly breaking. I dialled my mother's number and requested her to come and save me. She warned me that if I left, I'd start smoking, which would be bad for my upcoming operation. I contacted my therapist and asked her to get me out of there. She said exactly what my mother had said.

I was fucked and trapped.

Panic ensued. My bag was overflowing. I wasn't on anything. Nothing stood between me and myself. I felt like a small child terrified of creatures in the dark. Was I, nevertheless, the monster?

I discovered the stairwell. What about the nurse? There was no sign of him. Therapy? Therapy is a sham. I smashed those barriers with my head with the same force that Jimmy Connors used to hit his forehands down the line. There's a lot of topspin. Exactly on the fucking line.

Stairwells.

Every day, I'm this close to death.

I don't have any more sobriety left in me. I'd never be able to return if I went out. And if I went out, I was going to go out hard. Because my tolerance is so great, I would have to go out hard.

It's not like the Amy Winehouse narrative, in which she was sober for a long time before the first drinks killed her. She expressed something in that documentary that I agree with. She had recently won a Grammy and told a buddy, "I can't enjoy this unless I'm drunk."

I can't enjoy the concept of being famous, or rich, or even of being myself unless I'm high. And I can't think of love without fantasising about getting high. I don't have a spiritual connection that shields me from these emotions. That's why I'm on the lookout.

I had no idea what was going on when I reached fifty-five tablets each day, like the character Betsy Mallum in Dopesick. I had no idea I was addicted. I was one of the first famous people to go to rehab, and everyone knew about it. In 1997, I was on America's number one TV show and went to rehab, and it appeared on the covers of magazines. But I had no idea what was going on. In Dopesick, Betsy Mallum advances to heroin and dies—you see her nod out, grin, and die. But it's that smile that I crave all the time. She must have felt great, but it took her life. But that beatific moment is still something I crave, albeit without the death element. I'm looking for a connection. I desire that connection to something bigger than myself because I believe it is the only way to actually rescue my life.

I don't want to perish. I'm terrified of dying.

I'm not even excellent at locating the medications. Someone I worked with once introduced me to a corrupt doctor. I'd claim I had migraine headaches—actually, I had about eight doctors working on my fabricated migraines—and still had to sit through a 45-minute MRI to receive medicines. When things got very bad, I'd go to drug dealer houses. When the doctor died, his nurse took his place. She had all the medications, and she lived in the Valley, so I would go see her whenever I needed pills. I'd be scared the whole time.

"Come on in!" she'd exclaim.

"No!" "We're going to get arrested," I'd yell. Just accept the money and send me on my way."

She afterwards asked me to sit with her and do coke with her. I'd get the pills and, since I was afraid, I'd take three right away and drive home, high, to take the edge off the terror, which just made me more arrestable.

When I lived in Century City, I'd make excuses to go down forty stories to score. I was extremely sick and hurt at the time—my stomach hadn't closed yet, and I was alone throughout Covid... I had a nurse on staff who gave me medicines, but I wasn't getting high anymore. So I'd phone a drug dealer and acquire some more Oxy. This way, in addition to the meds I'd been prescribed, I'd be able to actually feel them. I was providing the guy $3,000 at a time, many times a week, because the street medications were around $75 each pill.

But I was caught more times than I was successful. The UCLA doctor in charge of my case became frustrated with me and informed me that he would no longer assist me. I couldn't blame him—everyone was frightened of fentanyl in the tablets and me dying as a result of them. (When I arrived at the treatment centre, I tested positive for fentanyl.)

This sickness... the dreadful thing. Addiction has damaged so much of my life that it's unfathomable. Relationships have been ruined as a result. It has wrecked my day-to-day existence. I have a friend who is poor and lives in a rent-controlled apartment. Never made it as an actress, has diabetes, is always concerned about money, and does not work. And I'd swap places with him in a heartbeat. In fact, I would give up all of my money, fame, and possessions to live in a rent-controlled apartment—I'd trade constantly worrying about money for not having this disease, this addiction.

And not only do I have the condition, but it is severe. In fact, I have it as terrible as it gets. It's always back-to-the-wall time. It'll kill me (I suppose something has to). When asked about his personal addiction, Robert Downey Jr. famously quipped, "It's like I have a gun in my mouth with my finger on the trigger, and I like the taste of the metal." I get it; I understand. Even on good days, when I'm sober and looking forward, it's always with me. There is still a weapon.

Fortunately, I believe there aren't enough opiates in the world to get me high. I have an extremely low bottom. Before I quit something, things have to get absolutely awful—big and horrific. I was virtually running the show Mr. Sunshine when I was doing it—writing it, acting in it. At home, I was taking notes for a writer on a script he had written. I had a bottle of vodka nearby. I made myself thirteen or fourteen drinks—but they were homemade, so triples. And I wasn't intoxicated after the fourteenth drink. So I stopped drinking.

I believe I'm now at the point with opiates where I'm in the same predicament. There simply aren't enough. In Switzerland, I took 1,800 mg of opiates per day and was not intoxicated. So, what shall I do? Call a drug dealer and demand all of the drugs? When I think of OxyContin, my imagination immediately jumps to having a colostomy bag for the rest of my life. That's something I couldn't manage. That's why I believe I'll be able to stay off opiates for the foreseeable future—they no longer work. And I could wake up after another operation, the fourteenth since the first, with an irreversible colostomy bag.

It's time to think of something else. (As previously stated, the next level is heroin, and I will not go there.) By the way, my decision to stop drinking and using drugs has nothing to do with strength—it simply no longer works. If someone walked into my house right now and said, "Here's a hundred milligrams of Oxy," I'd tell them, "It's not enough."

But the problem remains: I'm everywhere I go. I bring the troubles, the gloom, and the filth with me, so whenever I leave a rehab, I do a geographic and purchase a new fucking house. Then I live there.

And the first thing I used to do when I went house hunting, which is a hobby of mine, was rummage through the homeowners' medicine cabinets to see if there were any medicines I could steal. But you can't be a jerk about it—you have to take the correct quantity. You can't take too many or they'll find out. So you look at the date on the pill bottle—you want something that's a little old. You could take a bunch of them if they've been out of date for a long time. If it's brand new, you might only take a couple. On a Sunday, I'd spend the entire day visiting open houses.

When I was taking fifty-five tablets a day, I would wake up and have to find those fifty-five pills. It was like doing a full-time job. Maths was my entire life. I'll be there for three hours after I come home at eight o'clock. So I'm going to need four more. And then there's that dinner party. So I'll need seven people for that.... And all for the sake of survival, of not becoming sick, of avoiding the unavoidable, which is the detox.

I imagine the homeowners returning home after their open house and finally opening their medicine cabinet.

"Is it possible that Chandler... no, Chandler." Certainly not Chandler Bing!"

Instead than holding open houses, I'm having one built. I began the process because I couldn't finish a sentence about eighteen months ago. Things went from bad to worse for me. Doctors, my mother, and everyone else came in to care for me because I couldn't speak. I was completely out of it. I had no choice but to act. I had that $20 million Century City penthouse apartment where I was using drugs, watching TV, and having sex with my girlfriend of a few months. My mother and Keith Morrison were at the foot of my bed when we woke up one night after I had passed out and she had passed out. I wondered if I was in a Dateline episode. And if I am, why is my mother included?

My mother turned to face my girlfriend and said, "I think it's time for you to leave."

This literally saved my life.

My father has also saved my life several times.

When he assisted me in getting to Marina del Rey (after Jamie Tarses told me I was going to vanish in front of her eyes), I was terrified that I would never have fun again for the rest of my life. I called Marta Kauffman and David Crane after approximately three weeks to inform them I was sober and could return to Friends.

"When are you coming back?" they wondered. "We need you to return. It's going to be a lot of work. We have two weeks to start or we won't be able to finish."

But I was still quite ill. My father had caught the tone of the conversation and returned the call to Marta and David.

"If you continue to act this way around him," Dad threatened, "I will remove him from your television show."

I was glad for his being my father and doing the dad thing, but I also didn't want to be the source of the problem. They were simply going about their business; they had the number one hit TV show, and two of the key characters were set to marry. I couldn't just vanish. I simply wanted things to be alright. So I was transferred from Marina del Rey to Promises in Malibu and told that I would need more than twenty-eight days to recover—that I would need months.

A technician from Malibu drove me to the Friends set two weeks later. Jen Aniston remarked to me when I came, "I've been mad at you."

"Honey," I explained, "you wouldn't be mad at me if you knew what I'd been through."

We hugged, and I went about my business. I married Monica and was transported back to the treatment centre in a pickup truck led by a sober technician, at the peak of my highest point in Friends, the peak of my career, the famous moment on the classic show.

Let me tell you, not all the lights on Sunset that night were green.

I can't be effective in a relationship because I'm both trying to hold on and terrified of being abandoned. And that worry is unfounded, because in my fifty-three years and with all the lovely girlfriends I've had, I've only been abandoned once, many years ago. You'd think that all the others I abandoned would balance this... Nonetheless, she was everything to me. But the wise man in me sees it clearly: she was just twenty-five and just trying to have fun; we dated for a few months, but I let all my barriers down. I resolved to be myself once and for all.

She then dumped me. She had never made any promises to me. I was also drinking like a madman, which I don't blame her for. I had to see her at a play reading a few years ago since she played my wife.

"How are you?" she said before the reading, and I appeared to be fine despite the fact that I was in hell. I told myself, "Get out of there, don't engage, just pretend everything's fine."

"I have a couple of kids with my partner now," she stated, adding, "and life is good." "Are you dating anyone?"

"No," I replied, adding, "I'm still looking."

I wish I hadn't said that since it gave the impression that I was still looking after she dumped me. But it is correct. I'm still on the lookout. The play reading concluded, and she was no longer my wife; I got the hell out of there, and she still looked the same. I have confidence in God these days, but it often appears to be obstructed. But everything is obstructed by the medication I'm taking. These days, I wonder if Suboxone is interfering with my relationship with a higher force. One of my major issues, and the reason I've had so much difficulty getting sober over the years, is that I've never allowed myself to feel uncomfortable long enough to form a spiritual connection. So, before God can intervene and heal me, I fix it with medicines and drink. I recently took a breath work class. You breathe in this extremely intense, very unpleasant way for half an hour. You cry, you see things, and you become high. It's the best type of free high for me. Suboxone, on the other hand, completely eliminates the sensation.... Half of the doctors I've spoken with believe I should be on Suboxone for at least a year, if not the rest of my life. Other doctors say I'm not officially sober as long as I'm on it. (It's very tough to get all the way off it anyway, which is odd considering it's a medicine designed to get you off other drugs. When I was hooked up to an IV of it recently, the dosage I was receiving was 0.5 lower than it should have been, and it made me nauseous and worried, so I had to increase it back up. When you stop taking it, you feel dreadful.)

When you take heroin, the substance hits your opiate receptors, and you get high, and then it fades and you're no longer hitting the opiate receptors, and you're sober for a time, and then maybe the next day you hit your opiate receptors again, and you get high, and so on. Suboxone, on the other hand, functions differently, attaching itself around the receptor and refusing to leave, essentially destroying your receptors 24/7.

So, one of my beliefs concerning my inability to find happiness is that I've destroyed these receptors. Suboxone is replacing my dopamine. Dopamine is released when you like anything, such as watching a sunset, playing tennis and making a good shot, or hearing music you enjoy. But I'm very confident my opiate receptors are severely damaged, probably beyond repair. That's why I'm always a little disappointed. Like pancreatitis, perhaps if I left my opioid receptors alone for an extended period of time, they would heal and I would be joyful again. I've seen God, of all places, in my kitchen, so I know there's something bigger than me. (For starters, I know I can't grow a plant.) I know it's an all-encompassing love and acceptance that says everything will be well. When you die, I'm sure something will happen. I'm sure you're on to something fantastic.

Alcoholics and addicts, like me, want to drink solely to feel better. That was certainly true for me: all I ever wanted was to feel better. I wasn't feeling well, so I had a couple of beers and felt better. However, as the sickness worsens, it takes more and more and more and more and more and more and more and more to feel better. If you pierce the sobriety membrane, alcoholism takes over and says, "Hey, remember me? It's good to see you again. Now, give me exactly what you gave me the last time, or I'll murder you or drive you insane." And then my mind's fixation sets in, and I can't stop thinking about feeling better, combined with a wanting phenomenon, and what you're left with is a bruise that starts out one way and never gets better. Nobody has a drinking issue, then stops, then drinks socially, and everything is OK. The sickness is just getting worse.

According to the Big Book, alcohol is devious, perplexing, and powerful... However, I would add that it is patient. When you raise your hand and say, "I'm having a problem," addiction responds, "Well, if you're going to be so stupid as to say something about it, I'll go away for a while..." I'll be in treatment for three months and say to myself, "Well, I'm going to use it when I get out of here, but I can wait nine more days." The sickness is simply tapping its fingers. It's often said in AA that when you're in a meeting, your sickness is outside doing one-armed push-ups, just waiting for you to leave.

I've come close to death countless times, and the lower you go on the scale (death is the lowest, FYI), the more people you can save. So, when my life is on fire, I have individuals I sponsor, people who call me to help them with their lives. From 2001 to 2003, I had two of the happiest years of my life—I was helping people, sober, and strong. Sobriety also has some positive side effects. I was also single for a portion of it. So I'd go to clubs but not drink—the miracle had occurred for me. And, believe me, no one is more popular in a club at 2:00 a.m. than a sober guy who says, "Hi, how are you?" to a woman. I don't believe I've ever gotten laid more than twice in those two years.

But the sickness is not. You gradually cease attending all of the meetings you're required to attend. I definitely don't need to go to one on a Friday night...! And then, just as you're getting into that kind of thinking, alcoholism comes after you, befuddling, forceful, and patient. You're suddenly not going to any meetings. And you've convinced yourself that you know everything. This is no longer necessary for me. I understand.

Addicts are not necessarily evil people. We're ordinary people trying to feel better, but we've got this condition. When I'm feeling down, I think to myself, "Give me something that will make me feel better." That's all there is to it. I would still like to drink and use drugs, but I don't because the repercussions would kill me.

My mum recently told me she was proud of me. I'd written a screenplay, and she'd read it. I'd wished for her to say it my entire life.

"What about a little forgiveness?" she remarked when I pointed this out.

"I do forgive you," I explained. "I do."

I'm not sure if she can forgive me for everything I've done to her....

If I, a selfish, lazy fuck, can change, then anyone can. No secret becomes worse just because it has been revealed. At this moment in my life, I am overwhelmed with gratitude because I should be dead, but I am not. That has to be for a cause. It's simply too difficult for me to comprehend if there isn't.

I don't believe in winging it anymore. Scars are interesting because they tell an honest tale and are proof that a battle was fought, and in my case, hard-won.

I currently have numerous scars.

I fell into tears the first time I took my shirt off in my bathroom after returning from the hospital following my first operation. It really bothered me. I thought my life was coming to an end. After about a half-hour, I had the courage to phone my drug dealer, who proceeded to ask me what was wrong, as if he were a social worker or a priest, not a drug dealer.

I underwent my fourteenth operation three days ago—four years later. I cried once more. But I should get used to it since there will always be more surgeries—I will never be finished. I'll always have the bowels of a 90-year-old man. In fact, I've never gone through surgery without crying. Not even once.

But I've stopped calling the drug dealers.

My stomach is covered in scars, and all I have to do is look down to see that I've gone through a war, a self-inflicted war. Martin Sheen once turned to me at a Hollywood event—shirts were allowed, no, insisted on, thank God—and remarked, "Do you know what Saint

Peter says to everyone who tries to get into heaven?" When I looked at him blankly, the former president added, "Peter says, 'Don't you have any scars?'" When most people would say triumphantly, 'Well, no, no, I don't,' Peter says, 'Why not? Was there nothing worthwhile to fight for?'"

(Martin Sheen, like Pacino, Sean Penn, Ellen DeGeneres, Kevin Bacon, Chevy Chase, and Robert De Niro, are all members of the "Famous Club" I've encountered, which is an informal little thing you join when you're in an airport or at a function and someone else famous comes up and says hello as if we know each other.)

But the scars, the scars... My stomach is shaped like a map of China. And they fucked up. Unfortunately, 30 milligrams of OxyContin makes my body chuckle these days. Oral medications are ineffective; the only thing that helps is IV medication, which I clearly cannot take at home, so I return to the hospital.

I'd undergone a six-inch incision with metal staples in January 2022. This is the life of someone who has been given the big bad thing. And they won't let me smoke. It'll be a nice day if I don't smoke and nothing strange happens. When I don't smoke, I gain weight as well—in fact, I recently gained so much weight that I feared someone was following me when I glanced in the mirror. You gain weight when you become sober. You gain weight after you stop smoking. Those are the guidelines. As for me, I would swap places with any of my friends—Pressman, Bierko, or anyone else—because none of them had to deal with this huge dreadful thing. None of them had lived their entire lives with a brain designed to destroy them. I'd sacrifice everything to avoid having that. Nobody believes it, yet it is true.

But my life is no longer on fire. Dare I say it in the midst of all this turmoil? I've matured. I am more sincere and authentic. I don't need to leave the folks in the room laughing. All I have to do now is stand up straight and leave the room.

And preferably not right into the closet. I'm a different person now. A more honest version of me. A more capable version of myself. Sure, if I want a nice role in a movie, I'd have to write it right now. But I can do it as well. I am sufficient. I am more than sufficient. And I no longer need to put on a show. I've left my imprint. It's now time to relax and enjoy it. And discover true love. And a regular life. Not one that is motivated by fear. I am myself. And it should be enough, and it always has been. I was the one who didn't understand. And now I have. I'm a writer and an actor. I am a living being. And an excellent one at that. I desire excellent things for myself and others, and I am willing to work hard to achieve them. I'm still here for a reason. And determining why is the duty that has been assigned to me.

And it will be made known. There is no hurry or sense of urgency. The solution is simply that I am present and care about others. Now, when I get up, I'm curious about what the world has in store for me, and for myself. That's all there is to it.

I want to continue studying. I wish to continue teaching. Those are my lofty goals for myself, but in the meantime, I just want to laugh and have fun with my pals. I want to make love to a woman with whom I am deeply in love. I aspire to be a father and to make my mum and father proud.

I now enjoy art and have begun to collect. My Banksy painting was purchased at an auction in New York. I purchased it over the phone. I've never met him, but I want him to know that if there was ever a fire, I'd save my Banksy. I'm not sure he'd notice. (In fact, he'd most likely set fire to it himself.)

I've accomplished a lot in my life, but there is still so much more to do, which excites me every day. I was a Canadian boy who had all of his dreams come true—but they were the wrong dreams. Instead of giving up, I adjusted and discovered new dreams.

I'm constantly finding them. They're right there in the Valley, on the edgings and flashes that reflect off the water when the sun hits... just so.

I see God when someone does something nice for someone else. But you can't give something away that you don't have. As a result, I strive to improve myself on a regular basis. When those times arrive and I'm needed, I've sorted out my issues and do what we're all here for: to serve others.

CHAPTER 10

Batman

I never believed I'd be fifty-two and single, not running around with very short, attractive kids repeating stupid sentences. I'd taught them all only to make my beautiful wife giggle.

For years, I felt inadequate, but that no longer holds true. I believe I am just the correct amount. However, every morning when I wake up, there are a few fleeting moments when I am blurry, lost to dreams and sleep, and don't know where I am, and I recall my stomach and the scar tissue that comes with it. (I finally have rock-hard abs, but they're not the result of sit-ups.) Then I swing my legs out of bed and tiptoe to the bathroom so I don't wake... Well, no one. Yes, sir, I am completely single. I examine myself in the bathroom mirror, hoping to find something that will explain everything. I try not to think about the amazing women I passed up because of a phobia that took me far too long to grasp. I try not to think about it too much because if you spend too much time gazing in the rearview mirror, you will crash your car. Still, I find myself yearning for a romantic companion. I'm not picky—five feet two, brunette, as sharp as a whip, humorous, and generally sane will suffice. She adores children. Hockey is tolerated. Willing to learn how to play pickleball.

All I ask is that. A member of the team. If I gaze long enough, I can see my face begin to fade, and I know it's time to return to my patio and my view. Out there, beneath the bluffs and freeways and the meditation centre where I read my list to my sponsor, where the California gulls whirl and swoop, I watch the ocean ripple, slate grey with blue edgings. I've always believed that the water reflects the subconscious mind. There's beauty—coral reefs, beautifully colourful fish, spume, and reflected sunlight—but there's also something darker, sharks and tiger fish, and limitless deeps waiting to swallow frail fishing boats. Its immensity, and its might, are what most relaxes me. Large enough to be lost for eternity; sturdy enough to support massive oil tankers. We are little in comparison to its vastness. And have you ever tried to stop a wave by standing on the water's edge? It continues, no matter what we do; no matter how hard we strive, the ocean reminds us that we are impotent in comparison.

Most days, watching the water fills me with not only longing, but also tranquillity, thankfulness, and a greater knowledge of what I've gone through and where I am now. For starters, I've surrendered, but to the winning side rather than the losing side. I'm no longer stuck in a never-ending battle with drugs and alcohol. I no longer feel the desire to light up a cigarette to accompany my morning coffee. I've noticed that I'm feeling cleaner. Fresher. My friends and family have all commented on how brilliant I am, which none of them had noticed previously.

I read this in the appendix, "The Spiritual Experience," towards the end of AA's Big Book: Quite often, the newcomer's companions notice the difference before he does. I'm the newcomer this morning, like I am every morning out on the patio. I'm thrilled with, and inspired by, the "differences"—no alcohol, drugs, or smokes.... As I stand there, coffee in one hand and nothing in the other, watching the distant waves in the ocean, I realise I am experiencing my own wave within me.

Gratitude.

The wave of appreciation swelled as the light of day deepened and the water turned from silver to the palest aqua, till inside it I saw faces and events and little bits of flotsam that had been moments in my exciting life.

I was so fortunate to be alive, to have a loving family—this was not the least of my concerns, and probably the most important. I saw my mother's face in the water's thin spray and thought about her ineffable capacity to step up in a crisis, to take charge and make things better. (Keith Morrison once told me, "Throughout the four decades I've known your mother, her enormous attachment to you has been the core element of her life. She is constantly thinking about you. When things became serious between us in 1980, she said something I'll never forget: "No man will ever come between Matthew and me—he'll always be the most important person in my life." That is something you will have to accept."' And it's true—there was never a time when I didn't feel loved. Even in our darkest hour. If something is seriously wrong, she is still my first point of contact.) I saw my father's extraordinarily attractive face as well, and it felt fitting that I saw him as both my father and the Old Spice sailor guy, though that last vision had long faded to a far point on the horizon. I think about how they were able to be in the same room with me when I was truly unwell, and what kind of love that betrays. They weren't meant to be together. That makes sense now. So I'd like to reclaim all the pennies I've put into wells, wishing they were all together. They both got lucky and married the individuals they were meant to marry.

My sisters' and brother's smiles echo my parents', each of them beaming at me not only at a hospital bedside, but also in Canada and Los Angeles as I tried to make them laugh with my patter. They never dropped the ball, and they never turned their backs on me. If you can, imagine such love.

Images gurgled up from the turbulent seas, less profound but no less thrilling: the LA Kings winning the Stanley Cup in 2012, me in row seven shouting at the second line to keep the pressure on the boards. And my somewhat selfish thinking that God had them sail through the playoffs in a year when they only made it in the final days. I'd just finished a long relationship, and I'm sure the Kings went all the way because God said, "Hey, Matty, I know this is going to be a hard time for you, so here's something that will last three months and give you a tremendous amount of fun and distraction to make it better." After roaring through the playoffs like vengeful angels of death, the Kings defeated the Devils in six games in the finals, and that last game at the Staples Center was a blowout in a Stanley Cup game unlike any in two decades, LA up four-zip only a minute into the second period. I was at every game, even flying myself and some friends to the road games.

As the ice rink of my sports enthusiasm recedes, other faces emerge: the Murray brothers, my dearest oldest friends, with whom I developed a humorous manner of speaking that finally touched the hearts of millions. Hank Azaria, Craig Bierko, David Pressman... How their laughter was once the only medication I required. But I would never have met them, or gotten anywhere, if Greg Simpson hadn't cast me in my first play. You never know where one item will take you.... I suppose the lesson is to seize every opportunity because something good may come of it.

It resulted in something significant for me. When I opened my eyes, I was surrounded by my Friends friends (without whom I would have starred in something called No Friends): Schwimmer, for making us stick together when he could have gone it alone and profited more than the rest, and deciding we should be a team and getting us a million dollars a week. No lady has ever made me laugh as hard as Lisa Kudrow. Courteney Cox, for convincing America that someone so attractive would marry someone like me. Jenny, thank you for allowing me to stare at that face for an extra two seconds every day. Matt LeBlanc, who transformed the show's only stock character into the funniest character. They were all still a phone call away. I was the one who sobbed the most during the reunion because I understood what I'd experienced, and the gratitude I felt then mirrors the gratitude I feel now. Beyond those ideals, there was the entire team, the producers, the writers, the performers, the audience members, so many happy smiles. Friends would have been a silent film without Marta Kauffman, David Crane, and Kevin Bright. "Could this be more of a silent movie?" The fans, so many admirers who stuck with it and continue to watch—their faces stare back at me now, silent as God, as if I'm still on stage 24 in Burbank. Their laughter, which gave me purpose for so long, still resonates up these canyon walls, almost reaching me all these years later....

I remember all of the sponsors, sober buddies, and doctors who helped me not screw up the best job in the world.

I stare out at the lake and gently say, "Maybe I'm not so bad after all." Then I go back in for another cup of coffee.

Erin is always present in the house when I need her. I don't tell her what I've been thinking about out there, but I see in her eyes that she might have an idea. She remains silent because that is what closest friends do. Erin, Erin, Erin, Erin... She saved my life in rehab when my insides exploded, and she continues to do so every day. Who knows what I'd do without her; I'm not going to find out. I can tell she's craving a cigarette, but she doesn't give in. Find a friend who will quit something with you—you'll be surprised at how much it improves your bond.

The sun is higher now, and the perfect Southern California day is almost here. I can see boats in the distance, and if I squint, I think I see surfers relaxing in the calm waters. Still, this gratitude swirls around me, becoming stronger as more faces appear: characters from my favourite Woody Allen films, Lost, Peter Gabriel, Michael Keaton, John Grisham, Steve Martin, Sting, Dave Letterman for having me on for the first time, Barack Obama, the smartest man I have ever spoken to. On the breeze, I hear Ryan Adams' piano version of "New York, New York," recorded at Carnegie Hall on November 17, 2014. I realise all over again how fortunate I am to have been in this business, to have not only had access to extraordinary people, but also to have been able to affect people in the same way that something like Peter Gabriel's "Don't Give Up" affects me (let's not get into the video with him hugging Kate Bush; it's almost too much to bear). When I think of all the performers who take risks, I see Earl H.'s face, the good version, not the negative, and it's swiftly replaced by the face of my current sponsor, Clay, who has calmed me down so many times. I am grateful to all of the doctors and nurses at UCLA Medical Center for saving my life. I'm no longer accepted in that hospital after I was caught smoking there one last time. To Kerry Gaynor for ensuring that there would never be one last time. And, behind it all, the ghost of Bill Wilson, whose founding of AA saved millions upon millions of lives one day at a time, and whose organisation today refuses to shoot the wounded and always lets the light in for me.

I was thankful for dentists.... No, wait—I despise dentists.

I can hear children laughing somewhere behind me, further up the hill, which is my favourite sound of all. I take the pickleball paddle off the patio table and practise a few swings. I'd never heard of pickleball before, and I never imagined I'd be able to play any sport again. I'd given up swinging a tennis racket a long time ago, but this new Matty looks forward to days at the Riviera, hitting the bright yellow plastic pickleball.

Erin interrupts my daydream.

"Hey, Matty," she says as she walks through the kitchen door, "it's Doug on the phone." Doug Chapin has been my manager since 1992, and he, like many others in the profession, has frequently patiently waited for me to dig myself out of whatever hole I was in. Finally being able to work? Being able to write? Who knew such things existed?

My eyes welled up with tears, and the sea seemed further away, as if in a dream. So I close my eyes and thank God for everything I've learnt in this life; for the scars on my stomach, which only prove I've lived a life worth fighting for. What a gift it was for me to be able to assist my fellow man in times of strife and hardship.

Beautiful women's faces flash over my retina, lovely ladies who have been in my life, and I am grateful for them motivating me and pushing me to be the best man I can be. Gabrielle Bober, my first girlfriend, was the one who noticed something was wrong with me and sent me to rehab for the first time. Thank you, Jamie Tarses, for not letting me disappear.

Tricia Fisher, for initiating it all; Rachel's face; and the New York nurse who was a bright blazing beacon in one of my darkest days. I'm even thankful to the woman who dumped me after I'd opened out to her. And I'm grateful to all the lovely women I've broken up with because I was afraid—I'm grateful and apologetic.

Oh, and I'm also available.

I would not make mistakes based on fear in my next relationship, whenever that may be.... That much I am aware of.

With the sun at its peak, it's time to retreat to the shade. I hate leaving that vista; I'm not sure anyone will ever understand what it means to me, no longer an unaccompanied minor as I glide above the globe like that, about to be parented once more.

Life continues to go forward; each day is a new opportunity for amazement, hope, work, and forward motion. I'm curious if the A-list actress who has shown considerable interest in my new screenplay has yet to say yes....

I halt on the threshold as I walk inside. My life has been a series of portals between Canada and Los Angeles, Mom and Dad, L.A.X. 2194 and Friends, recovery and addiction, anguish and thankfulness, love and losing love. But I'm learning patience and getting a taste for reality. I return to the kitchen table and check my phone to see who has called. Not the A-lister, but there's still time.

This is how life is right now, and it's wonderful.

When I look across at Erin, she smiles back.

Being in a kitchen always makes me think of God. He appeared to me in the kitchen, of course, and thereby saved my life. When I empty my channel to sense God's greatness, he is always there for me. Given everything, it's difficult to believe he still comes up for us mortals, but he does, and that's the point: love always triumphs.

Man, the two most important things are love and courage. I no longer walk forward with fear, but rather with interest. I have an awesome support group who saves me every day because I have been through hell. Hell has distinct characteristics, and I want no part of it. But, at the very least, I have the courage to face it.

Who am I going to be? Whoever it is I will take it on as a man who has finally acquired the taste for life. I fought that taste, man, I fought it hard. But in the end admitting defeat was winning. Addiction, the big terrible thing, is far too powerful for anyone to defeat alone. But together, one day at a time, we can beat it down.

The one thing I got right was that I never gave up, I never raised my hands and said, “That’s enough, I can’t take it anymore, you win.” And because of that, I stand tall now, ready for whatever comes next.

Someday you, too, might be called upon to do something important, so be ready for it.

And when whatever happens, just think, What would Batman do? and do that.